The Eschaton

A Study of the End Times

The Eschaton

A Study of the End Times

By Wayne Clark

Pleasant Word

Pleasant Word (a division of WinePress Publishing, PO Box 428, Enumclaw, WA 98022) functions only as book publisher. As such, the ultimate design, content, editorial accuracy, and views expressed or implied in this work are those of the author.

The author of this book has waived the publisher's suggested editing and proof reading services. As such, the author is responsible for any errors found in this finished product.

Unless otherwise indicated, all Scripture quotations are taken from the New American Standard Version of the Bible. Copyright © 1960, 1961, 1963, 1968, 1971, 1972, 1973, 1975, 1977 by The Lockman Foundation.

ISBN 13: 987-1-4141-1129-2
ISBN 10: 1-4141-1129-0
Library of Congress Catalog Card Number: 2007908295

Contents

Acknowledgments

WRITING A BOOK seems to me to be a lot like having a child. It begins with a glint in the eye and grows into a subject-based love. As passion rises for the subject, focus increases resulting in knowledge and then conception. Once the creative life has begun, it gesticulates in you for a long and full term before it comes to fruition. The last trimester is pressurized and uncomfortable because you have given it all you can but you must still wait interminably. The book is in final production and there is nothing more you can do until it is ready.

And then it is delivered. With a mixture of excitement, anxiety and anticipation, it is taken from its packaging. It is there in your hands. You gaze upon it, holding it, caressing it with more love than you expected. It is "of you", created in your image, an expression to all the world of who you are. It may make you proud and/or embarrass you, but it is of you nonetheless. It will go out from you but you will not be there to explain it or make excuses. It will just have to stand or fall on its own. It is too late to turn back now. You will just have to live with it.

It (and you along with it) will be well received by some and rejected by others. And it will outlive you, reflecting who you were long after you are gone. Only as you hold it in your hands and count its "fingers and toes" do you realize the magnitude of what you have done. You look it over thoroughly to make sure all is well with it. You are suddenly more vulnerable than ever before. You can only hope that it will do well and prosper. But whatever happens, it is you and it is done. You cannot change it now. You hope people will receive it with grace, overlooking the little flaws and weaknesses choosing instead to be blessed by its strengths and the central nature of its being. You will always love it and others will politely fawn over it to please you, but you can only hope that it is genuinely worthwhile.

And then you understand that though it is an extension, a representation of you, its only real and lasting worth flows from the creative energy given it by God. It is what God put in it from conception that will endure and inspire those who encounter it. You take heart that God was there at its conception and nurtured it all along as it developed and grew in you. It is God who empowered it to be born alive and have being. And even though your genetic impact will give it character and style and expression, the only real life in it comes from God. You pray that God who began a good work in you will go with it all the days of its life. What you want is for others to see God in it, not just your contribution. So you dedicate this "child" back to Him in hopes that He can use it in His service. It is no longer really yours–never was, actually. It just has your name on it.

No child is created alone and its prenatal nurture and delivery involves a whole team of people to bring it safely to birth. And so it is with this present child–The Eschaton. I thank the Holy Spirit for revelation without which no man can understand truth or see God. I thank Sam Magruder who brought order and a professional look to these pages. He is a good friend and a tireless administrator without whom this book would not have gotten done. I thank Pat Anderson who numerous times edited every word, every line and every paragraph of this work, a tedious, time-consuming (but very necessary) task. Her mind is keen, her eye is sharp and her heart is generous. Great will be her reward. All of the above supported the work greatly in some way or another, but more importantly they challenged it forcing me to rethink and reconsider everything written for what, I am sure, is the betterment of it all. I also give thanks to the finest human being I have ever known, my beloved Nancy, who lets me be who I am while inspiring me to be more than I am. Finally, I dedicate this work to my mother, Mary Helen Clark. She gave me life and taught me to walk upright so that I might find God. And without that relationship, there can be no revelation.

Chapter 1

A Prologue

THE WORD "ESCHATON" is of Greek derivative and means "end times." From it we get the terms eschatology and eschatological referring (according to Webster) to things associated with the end of the world or the Second Coming of Christ.

Spiritual understanding and resultant belief is obtained, not through logical argument or intellectual persuasion, but rather through revelation. We are meant to use our intellect to find God, but only God can grant us revelation. It is God-given and unmerited. As such it is available to the old as well as the young, to the brilliant as well as the simple, to the "good person" as well as the flawed, to the pre-modern man and to today's scholars. Mostly, it comes to the receptive and the seeker. It is the special province of the Holy Spirit. The Spirit of God is like water. He comes down from above, takes the path of least resistance and freezes when He meets a cold reception. He is passionate to inform us but is a "gentleman," a respecter of our free will. He does not compel understanding or support the well-intentioned but misguided control issues of others.

The presentation contained herein will not prove to be persuasive to the unbeliever although it might add to the curiosity of the seeker. It is not intended to persuade the skeptic, the agnostic or the atheist. It is intended to provide support to the evangelical, the student of the Bible who requires that all truth find support in the Word of God to be believed. Its purpose is to show that the historically understood eschatology is well-supported in Scripture and that support is both

1

broad and deep, coming from many Biblical writers and from every age. It will present many scriptures in support of the claims made, often written out word for word. Other scriptures will just be referenced for further study.

The volume of scriptural support is intentional. Good people can disagree concerning how any particular scripture can be interpreted. Some of the scriptures offered may be rejected by the reader as not relevant to the claims made. The reader may, in fact, be right; the author is not infallible. However, it is the preponderance of the evidence that makes it strong. Dismiss a third of it or even half of it and you still have to deal with the rest of it. It is the accumulated effect of all of the scripture that makes the case, not the relevancy of any one scripture. Proof text without context is pretext. One can bend a scripture in support of several views when one ignores the context of the whole of scripture. This work attempts to bring to bear all of scripture so that, in the end, the patient student will have a solid picture of what is coming in the Eschaton.

The Eschaton is a Biblical survey of the end times, bringing to bear multiple sources including the patriarchal testimony of Adam and Eve, Noah, Abraham, Joseph, Moses, and David as well as the prophecies of Isaiah, Jeremiah, Ezekiel, Micah, Joel, Daniel, Zephaniah, Zechariah, Haggai and Malachi among others. We also see the support in New Testament leaders including John the Baptist, Matthew, Mark, Luke, John, Peter and Paul as well as James, Jude and their older more important brother, Jesus of Nazareth. In all of this we see evangelical support for the Eschaton that is both Old and New Testament and encompasses the writings of many, if not most, of the writers and key players of the Bible.

Good people can and do disagree about important issues. All of us hold our beliefs firmly in our hearts, as well we should. However, none of us is infallible and since we have all modified our understanding over time, we are likely to be more clearly illumined as time goes on. We see here on earth, after all, "through a mirror dimly." What is found in this writing is the accumulated understanding of one man's lifetime of study. It is sincerely and deeply held but is humbly submitted for the scrutiny of any who would find it useful. *When the Perfect comes, we will all see clearly for we will be like Him* (1 Cor 13:12). In all probability, we will all spend some time in eternity comparing fully revealed truth to our doctrinal positions and explaining to one another what we got wrong on our "term papers." We will, nonetheless, it is suspected, be glad that we did the profitable and important searching recommended by Paul, the Apostle to his young disciple, Timothy.

> *Study and be eager and do your utmost to present yourself to God approved (tested by trial), a workman who has no cause to be ashamed, correctly analyzing and accurately dividing [rightly handling and skillfully teaching] the Word of Truth. (Amplified Bible) (2 Tim 2:15).*

May this work be a blessing to its readers!

Chapter 2

A Biblical Survey of the End Times

A STUDY OF the Eschaton (the last days or the end times) must take into consideration a list of topics without which the concept makes no sense or fails to be fully comprehensible. Those topics function as an outline for this study and are as follows:

I. The Promise of a Messiah
    a. The Promise of a Messiah as Seen Prior to the Prophets
        i.   Adam and Eve
        ii. Noah
        iii. Abraham, Isaac and Jacob
        iv. Joseph
        v.   Judah
        vi. Moses
        vii. David and The "Son of David"
    b. The Promise of a Messiah as Seen in the Prophets
        i.   Isaiah
        ii. Zechariah
        iii. Micah
        iv. Daniel
        v.   Malachi
        vi. David

II. The Promise of a Preeminent Israel
   a. The Promise of Israel's Preeminence Given to the Patriarchs
      i.   Abraham
      ii.   Rebekah
      iii. Isaac
      iv.   Israelites
   b. The Promise of Israel's Preeminence as Revealed to the Prophets
      i.   David
      ii.   Isaiah
      iii. Ezekiel
      iv.   Micah
      v.   Zephaniah
      vi.   Haggai
      vii. Zechariah
      viii. Malachi
II. The Promise of a Re-gathering of All Israel
III. The First Coming of the Messiah
IV. The Despoiling of Sheol and the Opening of Heaven
   a. Soul Sleep and Sheol, the Place of the Dead
   b. Re-animation is Not Resurrection
V. The Second Coming of the Messiah–Tribulation and the Antichrist
   a. Daniel's Teaching on the Eschaton
   b. Jesus' Teaching on the Eschaton
   c. Peter's Teaching on the Eschaton
   d. John's Teaching on the Eschaton
VI. The Second Coming–The Timing and the Parable of the Fig Tree
   a. Signs of His Coming
   b. The Suddenness of His Appearance
   c. The Purging of the End Time Church

Chapter 3

The Promise of a Messiah

THE EARLY PART of this presentation may not be as provoca-
tive as the later sections wherein we study the Antichrist, the Second
Coming and the Millennial Reign, but it is just as important. It is
important to see God's consistent and frequent promises made to Israel
(and us) that He would send a Messiah and honor His commitment
to Abraham concerning Israel's preeminence and their re-gathering
down through the ages. These commitments are the foundation for
all the events that happen in the Eschaton.

The promise of a Messiah begins vague and undefined in the
Garden at the Fall, develops in the Abrahamic Covenant and in the
prophetic word of Moses. It escalates in intensity and definition
through the revelation of the prophets of the Old Testament, is
supported in the New Testament by Jesus, Peter, Paul and John and
finds final definition by the Book of Revelation.

The Hebrew word for Messiah (*Ha Mashiach*) is literally translated
"the **Anointed One.**" In Greek, it is translated "Christos." Because of
confusion in the Greek-speaking world with a more common usage of
"christos" in medicine and cosmetics, Paul clarified the understanding
of "Christos" for first century Gentiles. For the role of Jesus as the
Messiah, he substituted as his day-to-day descriptor the Roman phrase
"Dominus et Soter" meaning **Lord and Savior.** Although he drew
this phrase (Lord and Savior) from his reading of the prophets (2
Sam 22:3; Ps 106:21;Is 43:3, 11; 45:15, 21; 49:26; 60:16; Hos 13:4),
this was a term he and everyone in the first century could understand

because it was located on the back side of some Roman coins referring to the Roman emperor. It is this terminology for Messiah that has passed down to the Gentile church even to the modern era. It is also why Paul was often accused of speaking treason.

Jesus, for political reasons, having to do with the timing of His revelation to the world as the Messiah, referred to His Messianic work and calling by referring to Himself as the **Son of Man,** a term freighted with Messianic meaning taken from Daniel 7:13. When, at the "right moment in time," He acknowledged to the Sanhedrin more clearly His Messianic calling and His divinity, it resulted in His almost immediate crucifixion.

THE PROMISE OF A MESSIAH AS SEEN PRIOR TO THE PROPHETS

Adam and Eve

The promise of a Messiah to Adam and Eve in Genesis 3:15 represents the first mention of a Savior. In the midst of the catastrophic fall from grace, it is barely noticeable, but in retrospect it is certainly a good beginning. Paul points backwards to it in Galatians 4:4 when he describes Jesus as having been *"born of a woman."*

> *Gen 3:15 And I will put enmity between you and the woman, and between your seed and her seed; He shall bruise you on the head, and you shall bruise him on the heel. (NAS)*

Noah

God's very willingness to save the sons of Adam from their sins is evidenced by His raising up of Noah to rescue mankind from total destruction by the Flood. It shows His Messianic mindset.

Abraham, Isaac & Jacob

Abraham (like Noah before him and Isaac and Jacob after him) represents the Messianic Kinsman-Redeemer whose obedience to God and self-sacrifice empowers him to lead his people to the Promised

Land, rescue them from their enemies and rule over them as both priest and king. The people of the ancient world were largely tribal in nature and gathered themselves for leadership and protection under a strong central leader, a king, a suzerain lord. Even today in many Middle Eastern cultures and among primitive peoples around the globe, the tribal leader holds great sway over his people. He was/is usually a blood relative, hence a kinsman, and powerful enough to rescue you in times of trouble, hence a redeemer. This role was often handed down to the <u>first-born son</u> upon the tribal leader's death unless, like Reuben, Simeon, Levi, Ishmael, Esau and Manasseh, one was judged unworthy or God intervened for His purposes.

This Messianic tribal leader had to be kin (a blood relative) and also be capable of redeeming his people. Because Jesus was human, he could be our Kinsman. Because Jesus is divine, He has the power and authority to save us. That is why God had to become one of us. That was the stunning announcement of "Good News" God gave to Isaiah and to all of us in the 40th chapter of Isaiah's prophecy, but more on that later.

Isaiah, and later Paul, reduced this Messianic term to the more familiar term–<u>Redeemer</u>. Abraham, the prototypical Kinsman-Redeemer to Lot in Genesis 14, *"believed God and it was counted to him as righteousness."* This empowered Abraham to miraculously save Lot and his family. This central message of Jesus and Paul, that all salvation is based in relationship and all relationship is based in trust, had been revealed some 2,200 years before either of them was born and 700-800 years before the Mosaic Law when Abraham was saved by relation-based faith in God's word.

Joseph

Joseph tells us that his suffering was utilized by God to save Israel from starvation. He was functioning as Israel's Kinsman-Redeemer, a metaphorical type of the Messiah to come.

> *Gen 50:19-21 But Joseph said to them, "Do not be afraid, for am I in God's place? 20 "And as for you, you meant evil against me, but <u>God meant it for good in order to bring about this present result,</u>*

to preserve many people alive. 21 So therefore, do not be afraid; I will provide for you and your little ones." So he comforted them and spoke kindly to them. (NAS)

Judah

Judah and others filled the Kinsman-Redeemer shoes and functioned as "metaphorical types of Christ" in the Old Testament in spite of their obvious humanity and shortcomings. Judah was promised that the Messiah would come from his loins.

> *Gen 49:10-12 "The scepter shall not depart from Judah, nor the ruler's staff from between his feet, until Shiloh comes, and to him shall be the obedience of the peoples. 11 "He ties his foal to the vine and his donkey's colt to the choice vine. He washes his garments in wine, and his robes in the blood of grapes. 12 "His eyes are dull from wine, and his teeth white from milk. (NAS)*

Moses

Even Moses contributed to the Messianic promise pool when he was preparing the people for a long-term relationship as God's chosen ones. He saved Israel from God's wrath on more than one occasion. He promised Israel that God would send another significant Kinsman-Redeemer in time.

> *Deut 18:15-19 The LORD your God will raise up for you a prophet like me from among you, from your countrymen, you shall listen to him. 16 This is according to all that you asked of the LORD your God in Horeb on the day of the assembly, saying, 'Let me not hear again the voice of the LORD my God, let me not see this great fire anymore, lest I die.' 17 "And the LORD said to me, 'They have spoken well. 18 'I will raise up a prophet from among their countrymen like you, and I will put My words in his mouth, and he shall speak to them all that I command him. 19 'And it shall come about that whoever will not listen to My words which he shall speak in My name, I Myself will require it of him. (NAS)*

While numerous men and women have worn the Mosaic mantle in part down through the ages, only Jesus fulfills the calling of Moses, the man who parted the waters, defeated their enemies and represented them face to face before their God. That was the considered opinion of Peter, the Apostle who said:

> *Acts 3:18-25 "But the things which God announced beforehand by the mouth of all the prophets, that His Christ should suffer, He has thus fulfilled. 19 "Repent therefore and return, that your sins may be wiped away, in order that times of refreshing may come from the presence of the Lord; 20 and that He may send Jesus, the Christ appointed for you, 21 whom heaven must receive until the period of restoration of all things about which God spoke by the mouth of His holy prophets from ancient time. 22 "Moses said, 'The Lord God shall raise up for you a prophet like me from your brethren; to Him you shall give heed in everything He says to you. 23 'And it shall be that every soul that does not heed that prophet shall be utterly destroyed from among the people.' 24 "And likewise, all the prophets who have spoken, from Samuel and his successors onward, also announced these days. (NAS)*

David and the "Son of David"

David prophesied that the Messiah would sit on his throne. The Messiah was in Jesus' day often spoken of as the "Son of David." Those needing Jesus' healing cried out to Him as such and the crowds on Palm Sunday proclaimed Him to be just that. Even Jesus' enemies used "Son of David" in this manner (Mt 9:27, 12:23, 15:22, 20:30, 21:9). John demonstrates the validity of this when he identifies the Messiah in this manner in the Book of Revelation (Rev 3:7, 5:5, 22:16).

> *Luke 20:41-44 And He (Jesus) said to them, "How is it that they say the Christ is David's son? 42 "For David himself says in the book of Psalms, the Lord said to my Lord, "Sit at My right hand, 43 until I make Thine enemies a footstool for Thy feet. "' 44 "David therefore calls Him 'Lord,' and how is he his son?" (NAS) (Mt 22:40; Mk 12:36)*

Jesus is telling the Pharisees that although "son of David" (lower case "s") usually denoted that someone was a direct descendant of King David, Son of David (capital "S") was also an honorific title for the Christ (the Messiah).

Acts 2:32-36 (Peter said) "This Jesus God raised up again, to which we are all witnesses. 3 "Therefore having been exalted to the right hand of God, and having received from the Father the promise of the Holy Spirit, He has poured forth this which you both see and hear. 34 "For it was not David who ascended into heaven, but he himself says: 'The Lord said to my Lord, "Sit at My right hand, 35 until I make Thine enemies a footstool for Thy feet." ' 36 "Therefore let all the house of Israel know for certain that God has made Him both Lord and Christ– this Jesus whom you crucified." (NAS)

Peter is claiming that Jesus was that Son of David who was the Messiah.

Matt 21:6-11 And the disciples went and did just as Jesus had directed them, 7 and brought the donkey and the colt, and laid on them their garments, on which He sat. 8 And most of the multitude spread their garments in the road, and others were cutting branches from the trees, and spreading them in the road. 9 And the multitudes going before Him, and those who followed after were crying out, saying, "Hosanna to the Son of David; blessed is He who comes in the name of the Lord; Hosanna in the highest!" 10 And when He had entered Jerusalem, all the city was stirred, saying, "Who is this?" 11 And the multitudes were saying, "This is the prophet Jesus, from Nazareth in Galilee." (NAS)

Matthew is telling his readers here that the crowd thought Jesus was entering as the Messiah. They are greeting Him with the honorific title (Ps 118:22-26) and receiving Him in the manner prophesied concerning the Messiah's coming (Zech 9:9-17). The crowds on Palm Sunday responded to Jesus on that day as the long-promised **Messiah/Son of David** as prophesied by Zechariah in 520 B.C.

Zech 9:9-17 Rejoice greatly, O daughter of Zion! Shout in triumph, O daughter of Jerusalem! Behold, your king is coming to you. He is just and endowed with salvation, humble, and mounted on a donkey, even on a colt, the foal of a donkey. 10 And I will cut off the chariot from Ephraim, and the horse from Jerusalem; and the bow of war will be cut off. And He will speak peace to the nations; and His dominion will be from sea to sea, and from the River to the ends of the earth. 11 As for you also, because of the blood of My covenant with you, I have set your prisoners free from the waterless pit. 12 Return to the stronghold, O prisoners who have the hope. This very day I am declaring that I will restore double to you. 13 For I will bend Judah as My bow., I will fill the bow with Ephraim. And I will stir up your sons, O Zion, against your sons, O Greece. And I will make you like a warrior's sword. 14 Then the LORD will appear over them, and His arrow will go forth like lightning; and the Lord GOD will blow the trumpet, and will march in the storm winds of the south. 15 The LORD of hosts will defend them. And they will devour, and trample on the sling stones; and they will drink, and be boisterous as with wine; and they will be filled like a sacrificial basin, drenched like the corners of the altar. 16 And the LORD their God will save them in that day as the flock of His people; for they are as the stones of a crown, sparkling in His land. 17 For what comeliness and beauty will be theirs! Grain will make the young men flourish, and new wine the virgins. (NAS)

It was because they misinterpreted His First Coming to be the long-promised Second Coming that they were heard less than a week later calling for His crucifixion. We, in our day, also sometimes fail to understand that difference, resulting in a church that looks for salvation but not for sanctification. We want Jesus to save us from Hell, but we are less desirous that He would sanctify us, purge us from sin, discipline us and set us free for perfect obedience. (More on that to follow.)

The Promise of a Messiah as Seen in the Prophets

The prophets were better positioned than the Patriarchs in time and experience to understand more fully Israel's (and mankind's) need for a Messiah. By 800 B.C. the world had demonstrated its depravity over thirty-six centuries of human trial and failure to live up to the calling and promise of its creation in God's image. Israel had fared no better since its inception as a chosen and divinely delivered nation under Moses six or seven centuries earlier. Fallen man was incapable of obeying God and keeping His law.

Prophets are called for two purposes: they are sent "to afflict the comfortable and to comfort the afflicted." In the process, they sometimes foretell the future. They are sent by God to convict the world of its sin and to warn the world of coming judgment. Having delivered their sobering, devastating and horrifying pronouncements of judgment, resulting in repentance and remorse by God's people, the prophets switch hats and promise those repentant ones a divine deliverance.

In prophecy, redemption is sometimes promised in the form of immediate or near-term rescue from trouble, but sometimes the redemption is promised to arrive in the future lifetime of the people and of their descendants. Prophecy is often fulfilled in layers–some now, more later, and all ultimately at the end of time, the last days or the Eschaton. It is in this context that they foretell the future and in this context is found the promise of the Messiah in the prophets. What follows are some of the promises of these prophets of the Old Testament that are received as such by New Testament teachers and preachers including John the Baptist, Jesus, Peter, Stephen, Paul, Apollos, Prisca and Aquilla, the writer of Hebrews, Jude, James and John the Revelator. For this reason, they have been embraced as Messianic prophecies by Polycarp, Irenaeus, Athanasius, Augustine, Luther, Calvin, Wesley and countless others for 2000 years.

Isaiah

The prophet most renowned for his Messianic prophecies is Isaiah. Time after time, Isaiah foretells the coming of the Messiah. He often referred to the Messiah as God's "Servant." An example of his writing follows here along with New Testament support for the claim.

Isa 9:6-7 For a child will be born to us, a son will be given to us; and the government will rest on His shoulders; and His name will be

called Wonderful Counselor, Mighty God, Eternal Father, Prince of
Peace. There will be no end to the increase of {His} government or
of peace, on the throne of David and over his kingdom, to establish
it and to uphold it with justice and righteousness from then on and
forevermore. The zeal of the LORD of hosts will accomplish this.
(NAS)

Mary is told that her unborn child will meet this standard (see
Luke 1:32).

Isa 40:1-5 "Comfort, O comfort My people," says your God. "Speak
kindly to Jerusalem; and call out to her, that her warfare has ended,
that her iniquity has been removed, that she has received of the
LORD'S hand double for all her sins." A voice is calling, "Clear
the way for the LORD in the wilderness; make smooth in the desert
a highway for our God." Let every valley be lifted up, and every
mountain and hill be made low; and let the rough ground become
a plain, and the rugged terrain a broad valley. Then the glory of
the LORD will be revealed, and all flesh will see {it} together; for
the mouth of the LORD has spoken." (NAS)

Every Gospel contains a quotation of this scripture early in its
presentation in preparation for announcing the ministry of Jesus (see
Luke 3:3-6; Mark 1:1-6; Matthew 3:1-6; John 1:19-34).

Isa 9:1-2 But there will be no {more} gloom for her who was in
anguish; in earlier times He treated the land of Zebulun and the land
of Naphtali with contempt, but later on He shall make {it} glorious,
by the way of the sea, on the other side of Jordan, Galilee of the
Gentiles. The people who walk in darkness will see a great light;
those who live in a dark land, the light will shine on them. (NAS)

Matthew tells us that Jesus conducted His ministry from
Capernaum and from Galilee in fulfillment of this Isaiahan prophecy
(see Matthew 4:13-16).

Isa 61:1-2 The Spirit of the Lord GOD is upon me, because the
LORD has anointed me to bring good news to the afflicted. He

*has sent me to bind up the brokenhearted, to proclaim liberty to
captives, and freedom to prisoners; to proclaim the favorable year
of the LORD, and the day of vengeance of our God; to comfort all
who mourn, (NAS)*

This is the job description of the Messiah, according to Isaiah.
Jesus claims this job for Himself in His first address in Nazareth (see
Luke 4:16-20).

*Isa 52:13-53:12 Behold, My servant will prosper. He will be high
and lifted up, and greatly exalted. 14 Just as many were astonished
at you, My people, so His appearance was marred more than any
man, and His form more than the sons of men. 15 Thus He will
sprinkle many nations. Kings will shut their mouths on account of
Him; for what had not been told them they will see, and what they
had not heard they will understand. (NAS)*

Isaiah tells us the Messiah will be marred more than any man and
His form more than most humans. Jesus bore all of our iniquities on
the cross. He was crushed utterly and carried more guilt than any one
of us could carry in order to save us.

*Isa 53:1 Who has believed our message? And to whom has the
arm of the LORD been revealed? 2 For He grew up before Him
like a tender shoot, and like a root out of parched ground. He
has no stately form or majesty that we should look upon Him, nor
appearance that we should be attracted to Him. 3 He was despised
and forsaken of men, a man of sorrows, and acquainted with grief;
and like one from whom men hide their face, He was despised, and
we did not esteem Him. (NAS)*

The Messiah would be neither handsome nor physically attractive.
He would be a nobody and a man despised. His own people would not
"esteem Him." He would grow up where He would not be expected
to emerge. Jesus grew up in a backwater country and in a nothing
village. He lived as an exiled alien in Egypt, the lowest of the low.
He was acquainted with sorrows having suffered many Himself.

Isa 53:4 Surely our griefs He Himself bore, and our sorrows He carried. Yet we ourselves esteemed Him stricken, smitten of God, and afflicted. 5 But He was pierced through for our transgressions. He was crushed for our iniquities. The chastening for our well-being fell upon Him, and by His scourging we are healed. 6 All of us like sheep have gone astray, each of us has turned to his own way; but the LORD has caused the iniquity of us all to fall on Him. 7 He was oppressed and He was afflicted, yet He did not open His mouth. Like a lamb that is led to slaughter, and like a sheep that is silent before its shearers, so He did not open His mouth. 8 By oppression and judgment He was taken away; and as for His generation, who considered that He was cut off out of the land of the living, for the transgression of my people to whom the stroke was due? (NAS)

He was our scapegoat, falsely accused. He suffered for our sins and bore our punishment in an uncomplaining way, non-defensive like a lamb led to slaughter. His sufferings led to our healing, our salvation.

Isa 53:9 His grave was assigned with wicked men, yet He was with a rich man in His death, because He had done no violence, nor was there any deceit in His mouth. 10 But the LORD was pleased to crush Him, putting Him to grief. If He would render Himself as a guilt offering, He will see His offspring, He will prolong His days, and the good pleasure of the LORD will prosper in His hand. 11 As a result of the anguish of His soul, He will see it and be satisfied. By His knowledge the Righteous One, My Servant, will justify the many, as He will bear their iniquities. 12 Therefore, I will allot Him a portion with the great, and He will divide the booty with the strong; because He poured out Himself to death, and was numbered with the transgressors; yet He Himself bore the sin of many, and interceded for the transgressors. (NAS)

Jesus was crucified between two thieves (wicked men) but buried in a rich man's tomb (Joseph of Arimathea). He was totally innocent and yet God allowed Him to be crushed for our sins. By His obedience, He earned the most significant prize imaginable, to sit at the right hand of God (see Jn 12:37-43, 1:11; Lk 23:18; Mk 15:4-5, 27-28; Mt 27:57-60; Heb 12:1-2).

> *Isa 50:5-7 The Lord GOD has opened My ear; and I was not disobedient, nor did I turn back. I gave My back to those who strike {me,} and My cheeks to those who pluck out the beard. I did not cover My face from humiliation and spitting. For the Lord GOD helps me, therefore, I am not disgraced; therefore, I have set My face like flint, and I know that I shall not be ashamed. (NAS)*

Jesus did not resist when they spit in His face, scorned Him and slapped Him (see Matthew 26:67).

Zechariah

Perhaps no prophet is more to the point on the Eschaton (the end times) than Zechariah. He has several Messianic promises supported in the New Testament.

> *Zech 9:9 Rejoice greatly, O daughter of Zion! Shout {in triumph,} O daughter of Jerusalem! Behold, your king is coming to you. He is just and endowed with salvation, humble, and mounted on a donkey, even on a colt, the foal of a donkey. (NAS)*

Here we see a prophecy about Jesus' triumphal entry into Jerusalem on the first Palm Sunday (see Mt 21:1-9; Mark 11:7-11; Lk 19: 21-40; John 12:12-19).

> *Zech 12:9-10 "And it will come about in that day that I will set about to destroy all the nations that come against Jerusalem." And I will pour out on the house of David and on the inhabitants of Jerusalem, the Spirit of grace and of supplication, so that they will look on Me whom they have pierced; and they will mourn for Him, as one mourns for an only son, and they will weep bitterly over Him, like the bitter weeping over a first-born. (NAS)*

Zechariah sees the lamenting of the women of Israel who walked the Via Dolorosa (Street of Sorrows) with Jesus up the hill to Calvary and the piercing of Jesus' side to verify His death (see Lk 232:28; John 19:31-37; 20:27).

Micah

Micah was another prophet whose Messianic promise is supported in the New Testament.

Micah 5:2-4 "But as for you, Bethlehem Ephrathah, {too} little to be among the clans of Judah, from you One will go forth for me to be ruler in Israel. His goings forth are from long ago, from the days of eternity. Therefore, He will give them {up} until the time when she who is in labor has borne a child. Then the remainder of His brethren will return to the sons of Israel. And He will arise and shepherd {His flock} in the strength of the LORD, in the majesty of the name of the LORD His God. And they will remain, because at that time He will be great to the ends of the earth. (NAS)

Luke records how Jesus came to be born in Bethlehem, many miles from Nazareth, the home of His parents (see Luke 2:4, 5, 7).

Daniel

Daniel had much to say on the overall topic of the Eschaton, including the timing of the comings of the Messiah.

Dan 9:25-27 "So you are to know and discern {that} from the issuing of a decree to restore and rebuild Jerusalem until Messiah the Prince {there will be} seven weeks and sixty-two weeks; it will be built again, with plaza and moat, even in times of distress." Then after the sixty-two weeks the Messiah will be cut off and have nothing, and the people of the prince who is to come will destroy the city and the sanctuary, and its end {will come} with a flood; even to the end there will be war; desolations are determined. "And he will make a firm covenant with the many for one week, but in the middle of the week he will put a stop to sacrifice and grain offering; and on the wing of abominations {will come} one who makes desolate, even until a complete destruction, one that is decreed, is poured out on the one who makes desolate." (NAS) (see Luke 2:1-2, Luke 19:28-44)

The first sixty-nine weeks of years (483 years) referenced here are the time frame between the command to rebuild the temple as prophesied in Daniel and the First Coming of the Messiah and, specifically, His crucifixion. The last week of years (seven years) refers to the end time, the seven-year rule of the Antichrist just before the Second Coming of the Messiah. (For further Biblical support of this calculation, see Appendix II, section vi.)

Malachi

Malachi was the last recorded prophet of the Old Testament. He, too, had Messianic prophecies that were supported by the words and life of Jesus Himself.

> *Mal 3:1 "Behold, I am going to send My messenger, and he will clear the way before Me. And the Lord, whom you seek, will suddenly come to His temple; and the messenger of the covenant, in whom you delight, behold, He is coming," says the LORD of hosts.* (NAS)

Luke identifies John the Baptist as the messenger who prepares the way of the Lord in fulfillment of Malachi's prophecy (see Luke 7:24-28).

> *Mal 4:5-6 "Behold, I am going to send you Elijah the prophet before the coming of the great and terrible day of the LORD." And he will restore the hearts of the fathers to {their} children, and the hearts of the children to their fathers, lest I come and smite the land with a curse."* (NAS)

Jesus bears witness to John's role as the prophesied forerunner in both the First and Second Comings of the Christ (see Matthew 11: 13-14).

David

Although David is not usually counted among the prophets, he is widely recognized for being prophetic. Concerning the promise of a Messiah he had much to say that was supported heavily by New Testament teachers, especially Psalm 22 in which he describes events associated with the crucifixion to an extraordinary degree of accuracy, almost as if he is an eye witness. Some of his prophetic verses follow here.

David's Prophecy:

> *Ps 78:1-4 Listen, O my people, to my instruction; incline your ears to the words of my mouth. I will open my mouth in a parable. I will utter dark sayings of old, which we have heard and known, and our fathers have told us. We will not conceal them from their children, but tell to the generation to come the praises of the LORD, and His strength and His wondrous works that He has done. (NAS)*

David predicts Jesus' use of parables to speak to the people (see below).

Fulfillment:

> *Matt 13:34-35 All these things Jesus spoke to the multitudes in parables, and He did not speak to them without a parable, 35 so that what was spoken through the prophet might be fulfilled, saying, "I will open My mouth in parables; I will utter things hidden since the foundation of the world." (NAS)*

David's Prophecy:

> *Ps 8:1-2 O LORD, our Lord, how majestic is Thy name in all the earth, who hast displayed Thy splendor above the heavens! From the mouth of infants and nursing babes Thou hast established strength, because of Thine adversaries, to make the enemy and the revengeful cease. (NAS)*

Jesus claims that David's prophetic words above are fulfilled at the Triumphal Entry of Christ (see below).

Fulfillment:

> *Matt 21:15-16 But when the chief priests and the scribes saw the wonderful things that He had done, and the children who were crying out in the temple and saying, "Hosanna to the Son of David," they became indignant, 16 and said to Him, "Do You hear what these are saying?" And Jesus said to them, "Yes; have you never read, 'Out of the mouth of infants and nursing babes Thou hast prepared praise for Thyself'?"* (NAS)

David's Prophecy:

> *Ps 41:9 Even my close friend, in whom I trusted, who ate my bread, has lifted up his heel against me.* (NAS)

David predicts that the Messiah is betrayed by a close friend with whom he breaks bread.

Fulfillment:

> *Luke 22:47-49 While He was still speaking, behold, a multitude came, and the one called Judas, one of the twelve, was preceding them; and he approached Jesus to kiss Him. 48 But Jesus said to him, "Judas, are you betraying the Son of Man with a kiss?"* (NAS)

David's Prophecy:

> *Ps 22:1 My God, my God, why hast Thou forsaken me? Far from my deliverance are the words of my groaning.* (NAS)

Fulfillment:

> *Matt 27:46-47 And about the ninth hour Jesus cried out with a loud voice, saying, "Eli, Eli, lama sabachthani? "that is," My God, My God, why hast Thou forsaken Me?"* (NAS)

Jesus is not in despair. He has not lost faith in the Father's love for Him. That would be totally out of character for Jesus and even sinful, exposing doubt. He is praying the prayer of the suffering Messiah from Psalm 22. It is totally pertinent to His immediate and present experience. Let us continue with it.

David's Prophecy:

Ps 22:6-8 But I am a worm, and not a man, a reproach of men, and despised by the people. All who see me sneer at me; they separate with the lip, they wag the head, {saying,} "Commit {yourself} to the LORD; let Him deliver him; let Him rescue him, because He delights in him." (NAS)

David foretells the scornful mood and taunts of the crowd at the foot of Jesus' cross.

Fulfillment:

Luke 23:34-36 And the people stood by, looking on. And even the rulers were sneering at Him, saying, "He saved others; let Him save Himself if this is the Christ of God, His Chosen One." (NAS)

David's Prophecy:

Ps 22:16-18 For dogs have surrounded me; a band of evildoers has encompassed me; they pierced my hands and my feet. I can count all my bones. They look, they stare at me. They divide my garments among them, and for my clothing they cast lots. (NAS)

David predicts the presence of Gentiles (dogs) at the crucifixion as well as the disposal of Jesus' garments.

Fulfillment:

Matt 27:35 And when they had crucified Him, they divided up His garments among themselves, casting lots; (NAS)

The dividing of the garments and the casting of lots for His clothing should be clearly seen in the soldiers' behavior concerning

Jesus' clothes. "Dogs" is a Jewish euphemism for Gentiles. Jesus Himself used it in conversation with the Syrophoenician woman (see below).

Fulfillment:

Mark 7:26-30 Now the woman was a Gentile, of the Syrophoenician race. And she kept asking Him to cast the demon out of her daughter. 27 And He was saying to her, "Let the children be satisfied first, for it is not good to take the children's bread and throw it to the dogs." 28 But she answered and said to Him, "Yes, Lord, but even the dogs under the table feed on the children's crumbs." 29 And He said to her, "Because of this answer go your way; the demon has gone out of your daughter." 30 And going back to her home, she found the child lying on the bed, the demon having departed. (NAS)

David's Prophecy:

Ps 69:7-9 Because for Thy sake I have borne reproach; dishonor has covered my face. I have become estranged from my brothers, and an alien to my mother's sons. For zeal for Thy house has consumed me, and the reproaches of those who reproach Thee have fallen on me. (NAS)

David predicts that Jesus will find reproach even in his home town and even among his own family members.

Fulfillment:

Rom 15:2-4 Let each of us please his neighbor for his good, to his edification. 3 For even Christ did not please Himself; but as it is written, "The reproaches of those who reproached Thee fell upon Me." 4 For whatever was written in earlier times was written for our instruction, that through perseverance and the encouragement of the Scriptures we might have hope. (NAS)

In Romans (above), Paul claims that this Davidic scripture is fulfilled in Jesus. Historically, Jesus' brothers and sister did not follow Him until after the resurrection. They can even be seen as attempting to reason with Him. His response is to stiff-arm them publicly.

Fulfillment:

Matt 12:47-50 And someone said to Him, "Behold, Your mother and Your brothers are standing outside seeking to speak to You." 48 But He answered the one who was telling Him and said, "Who is My mother and who are My brothers?" 49 And stretching out His hand toward His disciples, He said, "Behold, My mother and My brothers! 50 "For whoever does the will of My Father who is in heaven, he is My brother and sister and mother." (NAS)

Perhaps His family wants Him to come home and desist from His revolutionary message. Jesus' response to His brothers is chastising, even aggressive in His resistance of them.

David's Prophecy:

Ps 34:19-20 Many are the afflictions of the righteous; but the LORD delivers him out of them all. He keeps all his bones; not one of them is broken. (NAS)

John says that the scripture above was fulfilled at the death of Jesus. None of Jesus' bones were broken in the crucifixion. The two men crucified on either side of Him had their legs broken by the Roman soldiers as was the custom when they wanted to hurry the death process.

Fulfillment:

John 19:31-37 The soldiers therefore came, and broke the legs of the first man, and of the other man who was crucified with Him; 33 but coming to Jesus, when they saw that He was already dead, they did not break His legs; 34 but one of the soldiers pierced His side with a spear, and immediately there came out blood and water. 35 And he who has seen has borne witness, and his witness is true; and he knows that he is telling the truth, so that you also may believe. 36 For these things came to pass, that the Scripture might be fulfilled, "Not a bone of Him shall be broken." (NAS)

David's Prophecy:

> *Ps 16:10 For Thou wilt not abandon my soul to Sheol; neither wilt*
> *Thou allow Thy Holy One to undergo decay. (NAS)*

Peter tells the crowd at Pentecost that this scripture was fulfilled in Jesus and only Jesus.

Fulfillment:

> *Acts 2:22-31 "Men of Israel, listen to these words: Jesus the*
> *Nazarene, a man attested to you by God with miracles and wonders*
> *and signs which God performed through Him in your midst, just as*
> *you yourselves know– 23 this Man, delivered up by the predeter-*
> *mined plan and foreknowledge of God, you nailed to a cross by the*
> *hands of godless men and put Him to death. 24 "And God raised*
> *Him up again, putting an end to the agony of death, since it was*
> *impossible for Him to be held in its power. 25 "For David says of*
> *Him, 'I was always beholding the Lord in my presence; for He is*
> *at my right hand, that I may not be shaken. 26 'Therefore my heart*
> *was glad and my tongue exulted; moreover my flesh also will abide*
> *in hope; 27 because Thou wilt not abandon my soul to Hades, nor*
> *allow Thy Holy One to undergo decay. 28 'Thou hast made known*
> *to me the ways of life; Thou wilt make me full of gladness with Thy*
> *presence.' 29 "Brethren, I may confidently say to you regarding*
> *the patriarch David that he both died and was buried, and his*
> *tomb is with us to this day. 30 "And so, because he was a prophet,*
> *and knew that God had sworn to him with an oath to seat one of*
> *his descendants upon his throne, 31 he looked ahead and spoke of*
> *the resurrection of the Christ, that He was neither abandoned to*
> *Hades, nor did His flesh suffer decay. (NAS)*

Paul also makes the claim in Pisidian Antioch that this scripture (Psalm 16:10) was fulfilled in Jesus.

> *Acts 13:29-38 "And when they had carried out all that was written*
> *concerning Him (Jesus), they took Him down from the cross and*
> *laid Him in a tomb. 30 "But God raised Him from the dead; 31 and*
> *for many days He appeared to those who came up with Him from*
> *Galilee to Jerusalem, the very ones who are now His witnesses*

to the people. 32 "And we preach to you the good news of the promise made to the fathers, 33 that God has fulfilled this promise to our children in that He raised up Jesus, as it is also written in the second Psalm,' Thou art My Son; today I have begotten Thee.' 34 "And as for the fact that He raised Him up from the dead, no more to return to decay, He has spoken in this way: 'I will give you the holy and sure blessings of David.' 35 "Therefore He also says in another Psalm, 'Thou wilt not allow Thy Holy One to undergo decay.' 36 "For David, after he had served the purpose of God in his own generation, fell asleep, and was laid among his fathers, and underwent decay; 37 but He whom God raised did not undergo decay. (NAS)

Matthew (as well as the other three evangelists) testified that Jesus was raised from the dead and that His tomb was empty. This fulfills the scripture that the Messiah's body would "not see decay."

Matt 27:62-28:6 Now on the next day, which is the one after the preparation, the chief priests and the Pharisees gathered together with Pilate, 63 and said, "Sir, we remember that when He was still alive that deceiver said, 'After three days I am to rise again.' 64 "Therefore, give orders for the grave to be made secure until the third day, lest the disciples come and steal Him away and say to the people, 'He has risen from the dead,' and the last deception will be worse than the first." 65 Pilate said to them, "You have a guard; go, make it as secure as you know how." 66 And they went and made the grave secure, and along with the guard they set a seal on the stone. 28:1 Now after the Sabbath, as it began to dawn toward the first day of the week, Mary Magdalene and the other Mary came to look at the grave. 2 And behold, a severe earthquake had occurred, for an angel of the Lord descended from heaven and came and rolled away the stone and sat upon it. 3 And his appearance was like lightning, and his garment as white as snow; 4 and the guards shook for fear of him, and became like dead men. 5 And the angel answered and said to the women, "Do not be afraid; for I know that you are looking for Jesus who has been crucified. 6 "He is not here, for He has risen, just as He said. Come, see the place where He was lying. (NAS)

Chapter 4

The Promise of a Preeminent Israel

EMBEDDED IN THE promise of the Messiah was another covenantal promise–that Israel would once again become the preeminent kingdom of peoples in the world. The coming of the Messiah would bring not only a Savior (Redeemer) but a King who would sit on David's throne and rule and reign in the earth. In this we can see again the dual Messianic natures of Lord and Savior. All the nations who come up to Jerusalem, His throne city, would not only bow to Him but also would honor and make restitution to His people, Israel. In order for this to come to pass, Israel must be re-gathered and restored in a day when Jesus is physically ruling and reigning in the earth. This can only happen in the Millennial Reign of Christ upon the earth after the Second Coming.

Between His ascension into Heaven (forty days after His resurrection) and His Second Coming, Jesus is not physically found on the earth, nor does He physically rule the nations. Even though Israel has been re-gathered after a fashion since 1948, it does not enjoy worldwide respect, honor and stature. Nor will the nations bring restitution to Israel until they do so at the command of Israel's king.

THE PROMISE OF ISRAEL'S PREEMINENCE AS GIVEN TO THE PATRIARCHS

Abraham

*Gen 17:6-8 "And I will make you (**Abraham**) exceedingly fruitful, and I will make nations of you, and kings shall come forth from you. 7 And I will establish My covenant between Me and you and your descendants after you throughout their generations for an everlasting covenant, to be God to you and to your descendants after you. 8 And I will give to you and to your descendants after you, the land of your sojournings, all the land of Canaan, for an everlasting possession; and I will be their God." (NAS)*

*Gen 18:17-19 And the LORD said, "Shall I hide from **Abraham** what I am about to do, 18 since Abraham will surely become a great and mighty nation, and in him all the nations of the earth will be blessed?1 (NAS)*

Rebekah

*Gen 25:23 And the LORD said to her (**Rebekah**), "Two nations are in your womb; and two peoples shall be separated from your body; and one people shall be stronger than the other; and the older shall serve the younger." (NAS)*

Isaac

*Gen 26:3-5 And I will multiply your (**Isaac**) descendants as the stars of heaven, and will give your descendants all these lands; and by your descendants all the nations of the earth shall be blessed; 5 because Abraham obeyed Me and kept My charge, My commandments, My statutes and My laws. (NAS)*

Israelites

*Deut 15:6 For the LORD your God shall bless you (**Israelites**) as He has promised you, and you will lend to many nations, but you will not borrow; and you will rule over many nations, but they will not rule over you. (NAS)*

*Deut 26:18-19 And the LORD has today declared you (**Israelites**) to be His people, a treasured possession, as He promised you, and that you should keep all His commandments; 19 and that He shall set you high above all nations which He has made, for praise, fame, and honor; and that you shall be a consecrated people to the LORD your God, as He has spoken. (NAS)*

*Deut 28:1 "Now it shall be, if you (**Israelites**) will diligently obey the LORD your God, being careful to do all His commandments which I command you today, the LORD your God will set you high above all the nations of the earth. (NAS)*

THE PROMISE OF ISRAEL'S PREEMINENCE AS REVEALED TO THE PROPHETS

There are two main themes in all of these scriptures. They are that (1) Israel will become visibly preeminent among the nations, and (2) it has not happened yet. Therefore, we can expect it to happen in the Eschaton.

David

Ps 47:2-4 For the LORD Most High is to be feared, a great King over all the earth. 3 He subdues peoples <u>under us</u>, and nations <u>under our feet</u>. 4 He chooses <u>our inheritance for us, the glory of Jacob</u> whom He loves. (NAS)

Isaiah

Isa 2:2 Now it will come about that In the last days, the mountain of the house of the LORD will be established as the <u>chief of the mountains</u>, and will be raised above the hills; and all the nations will stream to it. (NAS)

*Isa 54:2-3 "Enlarge the place of your tent; stretch out the curtains of your dwellings, spare not; lengthen your cords, and strengthen your pegs. 3 "For you will spread abroad to the right and to the left. And **<u>your descendants will possess nations</u>**, and they will resettle the desolate cities. (NAS)*

Isa 60:1-3 "Arise, shine; for your light has come, and the glory of the LORD has risen upon you. 2 "For behold, darkness will cover the earth, and deep darkness the peoples; but the LORD will rise upon you, and His glory will appear upon you. 3 "And <u>nations will come to your light</u>, and kings to the brightness of your rising. (NAS)

Isa 60:11-16 "And your gates will be open continually. They will not be closed day or night, so that men may bring to you the wealth of the nations, with their kings led in procession. 12 "For <u>the nation and the kingdom which will not serve you will perish</u>, and the nations will be utterly ruined. 13 "The glory of Lebanon will come to you, the juniper, the box tree, and the cypress together, to beautify the place of My sanctuary; and I shall make the place of My feet glorious. 14 "And <u>the sons of those who afflicted you will come bowing to you, and all those who despised you will bow themselves at the soles of your feet</u>. And they will call you the city of the LORD, the Zion of the Holy One of Israel. 15 "Whereas you have been forsaken and hated with no one passing through, <u>I will make you an everlasting pride</u>, a joy from generation to generation. 16 "You will also suck the milk of nations, and will suck the breast of kings. Then you will know that I, the LORD, am your Savior, and your Redeemer, the Mighty One of Jacob. (NAS)

Isa 61:4-7 Then they will rebuild the ancient ruins. They will raise up the former devastations, and they will repair the ruined cities, the desolations of many generations. 5 And <u>strangers will stand and pasture your flocks, and foreigners will be your farmers and your vinedressers</u>. 6 But you will be called the priests of the LORD. You will be spoken of as ministers of our God. <u>You will eat the wealth of nations</u>, and in their riches you will boast. 7 Instead of your shame <u>you will have a double portion</u>, and instead of humiliation they will shout for joy over their portion. Therefore they will possess a double portion in their land, everlasting joy will be theirs. (NAS)

All of these texts predict a preeminent Israel in the end times when Jesus is reigning on the earth as their King, their Lord and Savior, their Kinsman-Redeemer.

Ezekiel

Ezek 34:27-29 Then they will know that I am the LORD, when I have broken the bars of their yoke and have delivered them from the hand of those who enslaved them. 28 "And <u>they will no longer be a prey to the nations</u>, and the beasts of the earth will not devour them; but they will live securely, and no one will make them afraid. 29 "And I will establish for them a renowned planting place, and they will not again be victims of famine in the land, and <u>they will not endure the insults of the nations anymore.</u> (NAS)

Micah

Mic 4:1-5 And it will come about in the last days <u>That the mountain of the house of the LORD Will be established as the chief of the mountains.</u> It will be raised above the hills, and the peoples will stream to it. 2 And many nations will come and say, "Come and let us go up to the mountain of the LORD and to the house of the God of Jacob, that He may teach us about His ways and that we may walk in His paths." For from Zion will go forth the law, even the word of the LORD from Jerusalem. 3 And He will judge between many peoples and render decisions for mighty, distant nations. Then they will hammer their swords into plowshares and their spears into pruning hooks. Nation will not lift up sword against nation, and never again will they train for war. 4 And each of them will sit under his vine and under his fig tree, with no one to make them afraid, for the mouth of the LORD of hosts has spoken. 5 Though all the peoples walk each in the name of his god. As for us, we will walk in the name of the LORD our God forever and ever. (NAS)

Zephaniah

Zeph 3:19-20 "Behold, I am going to deal at that time with all your oppressors, I will save the lame and gather the outcast, and I will turn their shame into praise and renown in all the earth. 20 "At that time I will bring you in, even at the time when I gather you together. Indeed, <u>I will give you renown and praise among all the peoples of the earth</u>, when I restore your fortunes before your eyes," Says the LORD. (NAS)

Haggai

Hag 2:6-9 "For thus says the LORD of hosts, 'Once more in a little while, I am going to shake the heavens and the earth, the sea also and the dry land. 7'And I will shake all the nations; and <u>they will come with the wealth of all nations;</u> and I will fill this house with glory,' says the LORD of hosts. 8 'The silver is Mine, and the gold is Mine,' declares the LORD of hosts. 9 <u>'The latter glory of this house</u> will be greater than the former,' says the LORD of hosts,' and in this place I shall give peace,' declares the LORD of hosts." (NAS)

Zechariah

Zech 2:10-13 "Sing for joy and be glad, O daughter of Zion; for behold I am coming and I will dwell in your midst," declares the LORD. 11 "And <u>many nations will join themselves to the LORD in that day and will become My people.</u> Then I will dwell in your midst, and you will know that the LORD of hosts has sent Me to you. 12 "And the LORD will possess Judah as His portion in the holy land, and will again choose Jerusalem. 13 "Be silent, all flesh, before the LORD; for He is aroused from His holy habitation." (NAS)

Zech 8:20-23 "Thus says the LORD of hosts, 'It will yet be that peoples will come, even the inhabitants of many cities. 21 'And the inhabitants of one will go to another saying, "Let us go at once to entreat the favor of the LORD, and to seek the LORD of hosts; I will also go." 22'So many peoples and mighty nations will come to seek the LORD of hosts in Jerusalem and to entreat the favor of the LORD.' 23 "Thus says the LORD of hosts, <u>'In those days ten men from all the nations will grasp the garment of a Jew saying,"</u> <u>Let us go with you, for we have heard that God is with you.</u> (NAS)

Malachi

Mal 1:11 "For from the rising of the sun, even to its setting, My name will be great among the nations, and in every place incense is going to be offered to My name, and a grain offering that is pure; for <u>My name will be great among the nations,</u>" says the LORD of hosts. (NAS)

Mal 3:10-12 "Then I will rebuke the devourer for you, so that it may not destroy the fruits of the ground; nor will your vine in the field cast its grapes," says the LORD of hosts. 12 "And all the nations will call you blessed, for you shall be a delightful land," says the LORD of hosts. (NAS)

The number and specificity of these scriptures is overwhelming– too overwhelming to dismiss. Either they are literal and accurate or they are not. It is not my role or intent to convince the skeptic, but rather to point out to the evangelical (Bible-believing) Christian the sheer magnitude of the promise of Israel's restoration to pre-eminence. If they are literal, and that is my assumption, it is clear that they are not yet fulfilled. One may dismiss some on the basis that they do not actually say what I claim they say, but one cannot dismiss all of them. Since they have not yet been fully fulfilled up to now, they must point to a later fulfillment–to the Eschaton, the end of time.

Chapter 5

The Promise of the Re-Gathering of all Israel

THE ULTIMATE RE-GATHERING of all Israel back to God and the Promised Land is another Biblical requirement for and immediate precursor of the Eschaton. While some "re-gathering scriptures" speak mainly (even in some cases exclusively) of the return to Jerusalem of the Babylonian exiles in the sixth century B.C. under Zerubbabel, Ezra and Nehemiah, many (if not most) refer directly or logically to an ultimate re-gathering of God's people by God's hand for the purpose of kingdom restoration under the Messiah. This is why the 1948 re-gathering of Israel in Palestine has electrified Judeo-Christian evangelicals and fed an expectation of the soon-coming of the Messiah. Whether or not the 1948 restoration of Israel is a bellwether event as some believe, the Bible has much to say about a pre-eschatological re-gathering of Israel.

Deut 30:3-4 If your outcasts are at the ends of the earth, from there the LORD your God will gather you, and from there He will bring you back. (NAS)

Neh 1:8-9 Remember the word which Thou didst command Thy servant Moses, saying, 'If you are unfaithful I will scatter you among the peoples; 9 but if you return to Me and keep My commandments and do them, though those of you who have been scattered were in the most remote part of the heavens, I will gather them from there and will bring them to the place where I have chosen to cause My name to dwell.' (NAS)

Isa 11:11-12 Then it will happen on that day that the Lord Will again recover the second time with His hand the remnant of His people, who will remain, from Assyria, Egypt, Pathros, Cush, Elam, Shinar, Hamath, and from the islands of the sea. 12 And He will lift up a standard for the nations, and <u>will assemble the banished ones of Israel, and will gather the dispersed of Judah from the four corners of the earth</u>. (NAS)

Isa 43:4-9 "Since you are precious in My sight, since you are honored and I love you, I will give other men in your place and other peoples in exchange for your life. 5 "Do not fear, for I am with you. <u>I will bring your offspring from the east, and gather you from the west. 6 "I will say to the north, 'Give them up!' and to the south, 'Do not hold them back.' Bring My sons from afar, and My daughters from the ends of the earth,</u> 7 Everyone who is called by My name, and whom I have created for My glory, whom I have formed, even whom I have made. " 8 Bring out the people who are blind, even though they have eyes, and the deaf, even though they have ears. (NAS)

Isa 54:7-8 "For a brief moment I forsook you, but <u>with great compassion I will gather you</u>. 8 "In an outburst of anger I hid My face from you for a moment; but with everlasting lovingkindness I will have compassion on you," Says the LORD your Redeemer. (NAS)

Isa 56:8 <u>The Lord GOD, who gathers the dispersed of Israel</u>, declares, "Yet others I will gather to them, to those already gathered." (NAS)

Isa 60:1-4 "Arise, shine; for your light has come, and the glory of the LORD has risen upon you. 2 "For behold, darkness will cover the earth, and deep darkness the peoples; but the LORD will rise upon you, and His glory will appear upon you. 3 "And nations will come to your light, and kings to the brightness of your rising. 4 "Lift up your eyes round about, and see. <u>They all gather together, they come to you. Your sons will come from afar, and your daughters will be carried in the arms.</u>

Jer 23:1-4 "Woe to the shepherds who are destroying and scattering the sheep of My pasture!" declares the LORD. 2 Therefore thus says the LORD God of Israel concerning the shepherds who are tending My people: "You have scattered My flock and driven them away, and have not attended to them; behold, I am about to attend to you for the evil of your deeds," declares the LORD. 3 "Then I Myself shall gather the remnant of My flock out of all the countries where I have driven them and shall bring them back to their pasture; and they will be fruitful and multiply. 4 "I shall also raise up shepherds over them and they will tend them; and they will not be afraid any longer, nor be terrified, nor will any be missing," declares the LORD (NAS)

Jer 29:11-14 'For I know the plans that I have for you,' declares the LORD,' plans for welfare and not for calamity to give you a future and a hope. 12 'Then you will call upon Me and come and pray to Me, and I will listen to you. 13 'And you will seek Me and find Me, when you search for Me with all your heart. 14 'And I will be found by you,' declares the LORD,' and I will restore your fortunes and will gather you from all the nations and from all the places where I have driven you,' declares the LORD,' and I will bring you back to the place from where I sent you into exile.' (NAS)

Jer 31:7-9 For thus says the LORD, "Sing aloud with gladness for Jacob, and shout among the chiefs of the nations. Proclaim, give praise, and say, 'O LORD, save Thy people, the remnant of Israel.' 8 "Behold, I am bringing them from the north country, and I will gather them from the remote parts of the earth, among them the blind and the lame, the woman with child and she who is in labor with child, together; a great company, they shall return here. 9 "With weeping they shall come, and by supplication I will lead them; I will make them walk by streams of waters, on a straight path in which they shall not stumble; for I am a father to Israel, and Ephraim is My first-born." (NAS)

Jer 31:10-11 Hear the word of the LORD, O nations, and declare in the coastlands afar off, and say, "He who scattered Israel will gather him, and keep him as a shepherd keeps his flock." 11 For the LORD has ransomed Jacob, and redeemed him from the hand of him who was stronger than he. (NAS)

Jer 32:37-41 "Behold, I will gather them out of all the lands to which I have driven them in My anger, in My wrath, and in great indignation; and I will bring them back to this place and make them dwell in safety. 38 "And they shall be My people, and I will be their God; 39 and I will give them one heart and one way, that they may fear Me always, for their own good, and for the good of their children after them. 40 "And I will make an everlasting covenant with them that I will not turn away from them, to do them good; and I will put the fear of Me in their hearts so that they will not turn away from Me. 41 "And I will rejoice over them to do them good, and I will faithfully plant them in this land with all My heart and with all My soul. (NAS)

Ezek 11:16-17 "Therefore say, 'Thus says the Lord GOD,'" Though I had removed them far away among the nations, and though I had scattered them among the countries, yet I was a sanctuary for them a little while in the countries where they had gone. "' 17 "Therefore say, 'Thus says the Lord GOD,'" I shall gather you from the peoples and assemble you out of the countries among which you have been scattered, and I shall give you the land of Israel."' (NAS)

Ezek 20:33-38 "As I live," declares the Lord GOD, "surely with a mighty hand and with an outstretched arm and with wrath poured out, I shall be king over you. 34 "And I shall bring you out from the peoples and gather you from the lands where you are scattered, with a mighty hand and with an outstretched arm and with wrath poured out; 35 and I shall bring you into the wilderness of the peoples, and there I shall enter into judgment with you face to face. 36 "As I entered into judgment with your fathers in the wilderness of the land of Egypt, so I will enter into judgment with you," declares the Lord GOD. 37 "And I shall make you pass under the rod, and I shall bring you into the bond of the covenant; 38 and I shall purge from you the rebels and those who transgress against Me; I shall bring them out of the land where they sojourn, but they will not enter the land of Israel. Thus you will know that I am the LORD. (NAS)

Ezek 20:41-42 "As a soothing aroma I shall accept you, when I bring you out from the peoples and gather you from the lands where you are scattered; and I shall prove Myself holy among you in the sight of the nations. 42 "And <u>you will know that I am the LORD, when I bring you into the land of Israel</u>, into the land which I swore to give to your forefathers. (NAS)

Ezek 28:25-26 'Thus says the Lord GOD, "<u>When I gather the house of Israel from the peoples among whom they are scattered,</u> and shall manifest My holiness in them in the sight of the nations, then they will live in their land which I gave to My servant Jacob. 26 "<u>And they will live in it securely; and they will build houses, plant vineyards, and live securely</u>, when I execute judgments upon all who scorn them round about them. Then they will know that I am the LORD their God." (NAS)

Ezek 34:13-16 "And <u>I will bring them out from the peoples and gather them from the countries and bring them to their own land;</u> and I will feed them on the mountains of Israel, by the streams, and in all the inhabited places of the land. 14 "I will feed them in a good pasture, and their grazing ground will be on the mountain heights of Israel. There they will lie down in good grazing ground, and they will feed in rich pasture on the mountains of Israel. 15 "I will feed My flock and I will lead them to rest," declares the Lord GOD. 16 "<u>I will seek the lost, bring back the scattered</u>, bind up the broken, and strengthen the sick; but the fat and the strong I will destroy. I will feed them with judgment. (NAS)

Ezek 36:24-28 "For <u>I will take you from the nations, gather you from all the lands, and bring you into your own land.</u> 25 "Then I will sprinkle clean water on you, and you will be clean; I will cleanse you from all your filthiness and from all your idols. 26 "Moreover, I will give you a new heart and put a new spirit within you; and I will remove the heart of stone from your flesh and give you a heart of flesh. 27 "And I will put My Spirit within you and cause you to walk in My statutes, and you will be careful to observe My ordinances. 28 "And you will live in the land that I gave to your forefathers; so you will be My people, and I will be your God. (NAS)

Ezek 37:21-22 "And say to them, 'Thus says the Lord GOD,"
Behold, I will take the sons of Israel from among the nations where
they have gone, and I will gather them from every side and bring
them into their own land; 22 and I will make them one nation in
the land, on the mountains of Israel; and one king will be king for
all of them; and they will no longer be two nations, and they will
no longer be divided into two kingdoms. (NAS)

Ezek 39:27-29 "When I bring them back from the peoples and
gather them from the lands of their enemies, then I shall be sanctified
through them in the sight of the many nations. 28 "Then they will
know that I am the LORD their God because I made them go into
exile among the nations, and then gathered them again to their own
land; and I will leave none of them there any longer. 29 "And I will
not hide My face from them any longer, for I shall have poured out
My Spirit on the house of Israel," declares the Lord GOD. (NAS)

Zeph 3:19-20 "Behold, I am going to deal at that time with all
your oppressors, I will save the lame and gather the outcast, and
I will turn their shame into praise and renown in all the earth. 20
"At that time I will bring you in, even at the time when I gather
you together; Indeed, I will give you renown and praise among all
the peoples of the earth, when I restore your fortunes before your
eyes," Says the LORD. (NAS)

Once again the scriptural evidence is overwhelming in support
of a re-gathering of Israel in the time of the end.

Chapter 6

The First Coming
of the Messiah

ADVENT–THE WORD means "a coming" from the Latin *ad veneo*; i.e., to come. When we think of Advent we think of the forty-day season before Christmas when we celebrate and anticipate the coming of the Lord–that is, the First Coming of the Lord.

The prophets foretold the coming of the Lord, but they described it as a two-part experience. On the one hand, the Messiah was expected to eventually come as a warrior in the defense of His people and as a King to rule over them in a new kingdom. This event has come to be known as the Second Coming of Christ. Jesus promised to return "like lightning from one end of the sky to another" and angels promised the disciples that it would happen.

But the prophets also had much to say about a prior advent or "coming" of the same Messiah, one designed to cleanse us of our sins. Malachi, the last prophet of the Old Testament until John the Baptist, said it this way:

*Mal 3:1-6 "Behold, I am going to send My messenger, and he will clear the way before Me. And the Lord, whom you seek, will suddenly come to His temple; and the messenger of the covenant, in whom you delight, behold, He is coming," says the LORD of hosts. 2 **"But who can endure the day of His coming? And who can stand when He appears? For He is like a refiner's fire and like fullers' soap. 3 "And He will sit as a smelter and purifier of silver, and He will purify the sons of Levi and refine them like gold and silver, so that they may present to the LORD offerings***

41

*__in righteousness.__ 4"Then the offering of Judah and Jerusalem will
be pleasing to the LORD, as in the days of old and as in former
years. 5 "Then I will draw near to you for judgment; and I will be
a swift witness against the sorcerers and against the adulterers and
against those who swear falsely, and against those who oppress the
wage earner in his wages, the widow and the orphan, and those
who turn aside the alien, and do not fear Me," says the LORD of
hosts. 6 "For I, the LORD, do not change; therefore you, O sons
of Jacob, are not consumed. (NAS)*

It was because the men and women of Jesus' day were focused
on the Second Coming that they missed the First Coming. We, too,
are capable of overlooking our need for redemption and sanctification
because we are too fervently seeking a rescue; i.e., salvation. It was
not because of a lack of information, revelation or warning that they
(we) missed the first advent of Jesus. The Biblical prophetic record
is there for us all to see, if we will.

On Palm Sunday the week before Jesus was crucified, the Jews
welcomed Jesus to Jerusalem as the coming Messiah. They were
stirred by the recent reanimation of Lazarus and also by the image of
Jesus riding into town on the back of a donkey. They were tuned into
the prophecies of Zechariah in this regard. So they greeted him with
Messianic praises *saying, "Hosanna to the Son of David! Blessed is
He who comes in the name of the Lord! Hosanna in the highest!"* (Mt
21:1-9) What they were expecting was the Second-Coming Messiah,
but what they were getting was the First-Coming Messiah. When Jesus
disappointed their expectations, the same crowd was found five days
later crying out for His blood. They missed the First Coming because
they focused on the Second-Coming scriptures. They should have read
closer and listened better. The First-Coming Messiah's transport was
a donkey, the foal of a colt. The Second-Coming Messiah will come
on the back of a horse of war (see Rev 6:1-2 below).

*Zech 9:9 Rejoice greatly, O daughter of Zion! Shout in triumph, O
daughter of Jerusalem! Behold, your king is coming to you. He is
just and endowed with salvation, humble, and mounted on a donkey,
even on a colt, the foal of a donkey. (NAS)*

Here is the prophecy concerning Jesus' First Coming and the manner of His entry. What follows next describes the Second Coming of Christ and the manner of His entry when He returns.

*Rev 6:1-2 And I saw when the Lamb broke one of the seven seals, and I heard one of the four living creatures saying as with a voice of thunder, "Come." 2 And I looked, and behold, **a white horse**, and he who sat on it had a bow; **and a crown was given to him;** and he went out conquering, and to conquer. (NAS)*

*Rev 19:11-16 And I saw heaven opened; and behold, a **white horse**, and He who sat upon it is called Faithful and True; and in righteousness He judges and wages war. 12 And His eyes are a flame of fire, and upon His head are many diadems; and He has a name written upon Him, which no one knows except Himself. 13 And He is clothed with a robe dipped in blood; and His name is called The Word of God. 14 And the armies, which are in heaven, clothed in fine linen, white and clean, were following Him on white horses. 15 And from His mouth comes a sharp sword, so that with it He may smite the nations; and He will rule them with a rod of iron; and He treads the wine press of the fierce wrath of God, the Almighty. 16 And on His robe and on His thigh He has a name written, "KING OF KINGS, AND LORD OF LORDS." (NAS)*

This was what the Israelites of Jesus' day were expecting, because this was what they were hoping for. They were looking for deliverance, not sanctification. It wasn't as if they had not been given clear information about the First Coming of the Messiah. Both Isaiah and King David were explicit. The Messiah would be God's Servant and would suffer much to redeem us from our sins. A fuller description of Psalm 22 was already given in the chapter called **The Promise of a Messiah As Seen in the Prophets**. It is easy enough to see the suffering of the Messiah in these verses and easy to recognize them as a description of the crucifixion of Jesus of Nazareth.

Isaiah 53:2-12 2 For He grew up before Him like a tender shoot, and like a root out of parched ground. He has no stately form or majesty that we should look upon Him, nor appearance that we *should be attracted to Him. 3 He was despised and forsaken of men, a man of sorrows, and acquainted with grief; and like one from whom men hide their face. He was despised, and we did not esteem Him. 4 Surely our griefs He Himself bore, and our sorrows He carried; yet we ourselves esteemed Him stricken, smitten of God, and afflicted. 5 But He was pierced through for our transgressions. He was crushed for our iniquities. The chastening for our well-being fell upon Him, and by His scourging we are healed. 6 All of us like sheep have gone astray, each of us has turned to his own way; but the LORD has caused the iniquity of us all to fall on Him. 7 He was oppressed and He was afflicted, yet He did not open His mouth. Like a lamb that is led to slaughter, and like a sheep that is silent before its shearers, so He did not open His mouth. 8 By oppression and judgment He was taken away; and as for His generation, who considered that He was cut off out of the land of the living, for the transgression of my people to whom the stroke was due? 9 His grave was assigned with wicked men, yet He was with a rich man in His death, because He had done no violence, nor was there any deceit in His mouth. 10 But the LORD was pleased To crush Him, putting Him to grief. If He would render Himself as a guilt offering, He will see His offspring. He will prolong His days, and the good pleasure of the LORD will prosper in His hand. 11 As a result of the anguish of His soul, He will see it and be satisfied. By His knowledge **the Righteous One, My Servant**, will justify the many, as He will bear their iniquities. 12 Therefore, I will allot Him a portion with the great, and He will divide the booty with the strong; because He poured out Himself to death, and was numbered with the transgressors; yet He Himself bore the sin of many, and interceded for the transgressors. (NAS)*

As acknowledged previously, David is not usually counted among the prophets, but he is widely recognized for being prophetic. Concerning the promise of a Messiah, and as we have seen before, he had much to say that was supported heavily by New Testament teachers, especially Psalm 22.

Ps 22:1-18 My God, my God, why hast Thou forsaken me? Far from my deliverance are the words of my groaning. 2 O my God, I cry

by day, but Thou dost not answer; and by night, but I have no rest.
3 Yet Thou art holy, O Thou who art enthroned upon the praises of
Israel. 4 In Thee our fathers trusted. They trusted, and Thou didst
deliver them. 5 To Thee they cried out, and were delivered. In Thee
they trusted, and were not disappointed. 6 But I am a worm, and not
a man, a reproach of men, and despised by the people. 7 All who
see me sneer at me. They separate with the lip, they wag the head,
saying, 8 "Commit yourself to the LORD; let Him deliver him. Let
Him rescue him, because He delights in him." (NAS)

The opening words of Psalm 22 are the beginning words of Jesus'
prayer on the cross. Palm 22 is a "blow by blow" description of the
crucifixion, remarkable in its scope and detail. The Psalms were the
liturgy of the Temple and the synagogue. They were very familiar to
the Jews of Jesus' day. Here we see the Gentiles (dogs) and others
taunting Jesus from the foot of the cross. Here, and in what follows,
we see Jesus demonstrating His trust in God to deliver Him. Far from
being in despair, Jesus calls upon God for deliverance with confidence
(faith) that can only be strengthened by the sheer specificity of this
Psalm. Psalm 22 was written for Jesus for this very hour.

Ps 22:9 Yet Thou art He who didst bring me forth from the womb.
Thou didst make me trust when upon my mother's breasts. 10
Upon Thee I was cast from birth. Thou hast been my God from
my mother's womb. 11 Be not far from me, for trouble is near; for
there is none to help. 12 Many bulls have surrounded me; strong
bulls of Bashan have encircled me. 13 They open wide their mouth
at me, as a ravening and a roaring lion. 14 I am poured out like
water, and all my bones are out of joint. My heart is like wax. It is
melted within me. 15 My strength is dried up like a potsherd, and
my tongue cleaves to my jaws; and Thou dost lay me in the dust of
death. 16 For dogs have surrounded me; a band of evildoers has
encompassed me. They pierced my hands and my feet. 17 I can
count all my bones. They look, they stare at me. 18 They divide my
garments among them, and for my clothing they cast lots. (NAS)

Not only does this Psalm of David, written 1000 years before
the crucifixion, give us an extraordinary summary of Jesus' medical

condition on Golgotha, but it tells us minute details about things such as how Jesus' clothes would be disposed of by His crucifiers.

David understood that the Messiah would die. He spoke of it in Psalm 16:10. We know David is referring to the Messiah (Thy Holy One) because both Peter and Paul say so in sermons to Jews. (Acts 2:27; 13:35)

> *Ps 16:10 For Thou wilt not abandon my soul to Sheol; neither wilt Thou allow Thy Holy One to undergo decay. (NAS)*

Chapter 7

The Despoiling of Sheol and the Opening of Heaven

JESUS DID NOT come to save only the disciples of the first century. He came to save all men in every age, including the time before He was born. How this was accomplished shows that God knows how to bring all people - in every age, on every continent, in any circumstance - to Jesus for salvation. The men and women who started the modern Chinese house church movement testify that Jesus appeared to them and personally evangelized them. Testimonies of this can be found in the book The Heavenly Man by Brother Yun, one of its founders of that movement.

The Old Testament has numerous records of Theophanes (appearances of God to men) as well as Christophanes (the appearance of Jesus to men). The book of Hebrews in chapter 7 suggests that Melchizedek's meeting with Abraham was a Christophane. God's visit with Abraham on His way to destroy Sodom and Gomorrah was clearly a Theophane. God will make His salvation available to all people groups in every age in every place by methods of His own choosing. The despoiling of Sheol is another example of this principle.

Before the Resurrection, all of the souls of the dead went to Sheol. Jesus was no exception. When He died, His body lay in the tomb, but His Spirit went to Sheol as would the soul of any other human. Hebrews tells us that Jesus was tested in every way and in everything in which we are tested. He shared all of our experiences, trials and difficulties.

Heb 2:18 For <u>since He Himself was tempted (tested)</u> in that which He has suffered, He is able to come to the aid of those who are tempted. (NAS)

Heb 4:15-16 For we do not have a high priest who cannot sympathize with our weaknesses, but <u>One who has been tempted (tested) in all things as we are</u>, yet without sin. 16 Let us therefore draw near with confidence to the throne of grace, that we may receive mercy and may find grace to help in time of need. (NAS)

In going to Sheol, Jesus entered the land of the dead, the realm of Satan. Sheol was, and is, Satan's "trophy room" containing the millions he has tracked, deceived, captured and killed like some ruthless hunter of big game. At the end of time and after the final judgment, death and Sheol (Hades) will be thrown into the Lake of Fire, that is, into Hell (Rev 20:14). It was to get Jesus into Sheol that Satan had orchestrated the death of Jesus on the cross, that he might get him into his realm of death and, therefore, into his total and cruel control. But as we shall see, it was Satan who was defeated in Sheol, not Jesus.

Before we go on to those details, let's first talk about what sort of place was Sheol and about the condition or state of the dead in Sheol. Sheol (Hades in Greek) is not to be confused with either Heaven or Hell. Jews (and other ancients) who developed a belief in an afterlife believed that Sheol was divided into areas, including subsections called the Abyss (a prison for angels) and Paradise (the place for righteous dead). Paradise was the name of the section of Sheol where the righteous dead "slept" and was also referred to as the bosom of Abraham. Paradise is a Persian word meaning "garden of delights" or "Eden." They believed (and the Bible supports) that initially all the dead went to Sheol and that there they **"slept."** All Biblical references to Sheol (Hades) describe it as a place of sleep or mindless dreaming. Jesus taught and spoke from this same perspective. He believed in the concept of "soul sleep."

John 11:11-14 This He said, and after that He said to them, <u>"Our friend Lazarus has fallen asleep</u>; but I go, that I may awaken him *out of sleep." The disciples therefore said to Him, "Lord, if he has fallen asleep, he will recover." Now Jesus had spoken of his death, but they thought that He was speaking of literal sleep. Then Jesus therefore said to them plainly, "Lazarus is dead. (NAS)*

SOUL SLEEP IN SHEOL—THE PLACE OF THE DEAD

Every man must die and face the Judge of all the earth to account for his sins. The Bible speaks against reincarnation. Each person dies one time and then comes to judgment. There is, therefore, no second chance of salvation after death

Heb 9:27 And in as much as it is appointed for men to die once and after this comes judgment. (NAS)

Before Jesus opened the gates of Heaven for us by His death and Resurrection, all mankind went to Sheol when they died. Since the Resurrection of Jesus, the **righteous dead** (the born again ones) go immediately into the presence of God at the moment of their death and, more importantly, into the presence of Jesus, the Christ.

*2 Cor 5:6-10 Therefore, being always of good courage, and knowing that **while we are at home in the body we are absent from the Lord**— 7 for we walk by faith, not by sight— 8 we are of good courage, I say, and prefer rather **to be absent from the body and to be at home with the Lord**. 9 Therefore also we have as our ambition, whether at home or absent, to be pleasing to Him. 10 For we must all appear before the judgment seat of Christ, that each one may be recompensed for his deeds in the body, according to what he has done, whether good or bad. (NAS)*

At the judgment seat, all of us will be found guilty of sin, but those of us who have our names written into the Lamb's Book of Life will not be judged according to our deeds, but according to Jesus' righteousness. Satan accuses us to God and justifiably so. We are sinners. But Jesus imparts His righteousness to us. He gives us His bloodstained "cloak" through which God cannot see our sins. His righteousness not only is imparted to us **(given as a gift)** but is imputed to us. That is, the blood of Jesus causes us to become like Him and God will remember our sins no more.

Heb 8:12 "For I will be merciful to their iniquities, and I will remember their sins no more." (NAS)

The **unrighteous dead** still go to Sheol where they "sleep" until the end of time. As stated previously, Sheol is the Old Testament place of the dead. It is sometimes in the scriptures referred to as a prison, a pit, the grave or a place of sleep or mindless dreaming. The Greek name for it is "Hades" (not to be confused with Hell which is another place altogether).

*Ps 146:2-4 I will praise the LORD while I live; **I will sing praises to my God while I have my being**. 3 Do not trust in princes, in mortal man, in whom there is no salvation. 4 His spirit departs, he returns to the earth; **in that very day his thoughts perish.** (NAS)*

Death as a condition of sleep ("soul sleep") or mindless dreaming is not received by all believers over time, so an explanation with Biblical support is offered here. Sleep as a euphemism for death is common in both the Old and New Testaments. Job complains to God that if God allows him to go down into Sheol, he (Job) will not be capable of praising God. The theology of Job and most other Old Testament men and women held that there was no conscious moment in the grave.

*Job 14:12 So man lies down and does not rise. **Until the heavens be no more,** He will not awake nor be aroused out of his sleep. (NAS)*

*Eccl 9:5-11 For the living know they will die; but **the dead do not know anything**, nor have they any longer a reward, **for their memory is forgotten**. 6 **Indeed their love, their hate, and their zeal have already perished**, and they will no longer have a share in all that is done under the sun. 7 Go then, eat your bread in happiness, and drink your wine with a cheerful heart; for God has already approved your works. 8 Let your clothes be white all the time, and let not oil be lacking on your head. 9 Enjoy life with the* *woman whom you love all the days of your fleeting life which He has given to you under the sun; for this is your reward in life, and in your toil in which you have labored under the sun. 10 Whatever your hand finds to do, verily, do it with all your might; **for there is no activity or planning or knowledge or wisdom in Sheol where you are going**. (NAS)*

*Job 14:10-14 "But man dies and lies prostrate. Man expires, and where is he? 11 "**As water evaporates from the sea, and a river becomes parched and dried up, 12 So man lies down and does not rise**. Until the heavens be no more, **He will not awake nor be aroused out of his sleep.** 13 "Oh that Thou wouldst hide me in Sheol, that Thou wouldst conceal me until Thy wrath returns to Thee, that Thou wouldst set a limit for me and remember me! 14 "If a man dies, will he live again? All the days of my struggle I will wait, until my change comes. (NAS)*

Job does not expect to know anything or be aware while he is in Sheol, but he does not think that Sheol is his final end. Job's high theology expects an afterlife somehow and sometime after Sheol when he once again has "flesh" and eyes. He sees Sheol, the place of the dead, as a temporary place or state of sleep.

Job 19:26-27 "Even after my skin is destroyed, yet from my flesh I shall see God; 27 whom I myself shall behold, and whom my eyes shall see and not another. My heart faints within me. (NAS)

Job is not the only Old Testament man who believed in Sheol as a place of death and death as a condition of sleep. Nor was this belief limited to the Old Testament. As we shall see, Matthew, Luke, Peter, Jesus and Paul held the same view in the New Testament.

*Ps 13:3 Consider and answer me, O LORD, my God; Enlighten my eyes, **lest I sleep the sleep of death.** (NAS)*

*Is 38:18 For Sheol cannot thank thee. Death cannot praise thee. **Those who go down to the pit cannot hope** for thy faithfulness." (NAS)*

*Jer 51:39 (**Concerning the judgment of Babylon**) When they become heated up, I shall serve them their banquet and make them drunk, that they may become jubilant and **may sleep a perpetual sleep and not wake up**," declares the LORD.* (NAS)

*Dan 12:2-3 "And many of those **who sleep in the dust of the ground** will awake, these to everlasting life, but the others to disgrace and everlasting contempt.* (NAS)

*Matt 27:49-53 And Jesus cried out again with a loud voice, and yielded up His spirit. 51 And behold, the veil of the temple was torn in two from top to bottom, and the earth shook; and the rocks were split, 52 **and the tombs were opened; and many bodies of the saints who had fallen asleep were raised; 53 and coming out of the tombs after His resurrection they entered the holy city and appeared to many.*** (NAS)

*Acts 13:36-37 "For David, after he had served the purpose of God in his own generation, **fell asleep, and was laid among his fathers, and underwent decay;** 37 but He whom God raised did not undergo decay.* (NAS)

*1 Cor 15:6 After that He appeared to more than five hundred brethren at one time, most of whom remain until now, but **some have fallen asleep.*** (NAS)

*1 Cor 11:28-30 For he who eats and drinks, eats and drinks judgment to himself, if he does not judge the body rightly. 30 For this reason many among you are weak and sick, and **a number sleep***. (NAS)

*1 Cor 15:16-26 For if the dead are not raised, not even Christ has been raised; 17 and if Christ has not been raised, your faith is worthless; you are still in your sins. 18 **Then those also who have fallen asleep in Christ have perished.** 19 If we have hoped in Christ in this life only, we are of all men most to be pitied. 20 But **now Christ has been raised from the dead, the first fruits of those who are asleep.** 21 For since by a man came death, by a man also came the resurrection of the dead. 22 For as in Adam* *all die, so also in Christ all shall be made alive. 23 But each in his own order: Christ the first fruits, after that those who are Christ's at His coming, 24 then comes the end, when He delivers up the kingdom to the God and Father, when He has abolished all rule and all authority and power. 25 For He must reign until He has put all His enemies under His feet. 26 The last enemy that will be abolished is death. (NAS)*

*1 Cor 15:51-52 Behold, I tell you a mystery; **we shall not all sleep, but we shall all be changed**, 52 in a moment, in the twinkling of an eye, at the last trumpet; for the trumpet will sound, and **the dead will be raised imperishable**, and we shall be changed. (NAS)*

*1 Thess 4:13-18 But we do not want you to be uninformed, brethren, **about those who are asleep, that you may not grieve, as do the rest who have no hope**. 14 For if we believe that Jesus died and rose again, even so God will bring with Him those who have fallen asleep in Jesus. 15 For this we say to you by the word of the Lord, **that we who are alive, and remain until the coming of the Lord, shall not precede those who have fallen asleep**. 16 For the Lord Himself will descend from heaven with a shout, with the voice of the archangel, and with the trumpet of God; and the dead in Christ shall rise first. 17 Then we who are alive and remain shall be caught up together with them in the clouds to meet the Lord in the air, and thus we shall always be with the Lord. 18 Therefore comfort one another with these words. (NAS)*

*2 Peter 3:3-4 Know this first of all, that in the last days mockers will come with their mocking, following after their own lusts, 4 and saying, "Where is the promise of His coming? **For ever since the fathers fell asleep,** all continues just as it was from the beginning of creation." (NAS)*

David, Solomon and Isaiah also describe Sheol as a vague dream state or a place of unconsciousness (Ps 6:4-6; 31:17; Eccl 9:10; Is 38:18).

Jesus referred to Lazarus as being asleep when he died. When the disciples misunderstood the terminology, Jesus tells them plainly that *"Lazarus has died."* Jesus pointedly waits four days until Lazarus is stinking before He goes to wake him from the dead. He wants it to be clear that we all know Lazarus has died (John 11:11-15).

REANIMATION IS NOT RESURRECTION

There is a significant difference between resurrection and reanimation. Only Jesus has been resurrected from the dead so far. The rest of the righteous dead will be resurrected and receive their glorified bodies at the Second Coming. Lazarus and all others in the Bible who were "raised from the dead" were reanimated in their physical bodies and had to die again later. That is not true resurrection. Logic defends "soul sleep" for these people. Are we to suppose that these many people were called back from Heaven or Hell? The gates of Heaven were closed to all men before the death and resurrection of Jesus, so they weren't there. Are we to think that Lazarus and the synagogue official's daughter and Dorcas the widow of Nain's son, etc. had gone to Hell, the lake of fire, the place of eternal damnation? No, they were called back from Sheol, the place of the dead.

Since the fall of Adam and Eve in the Garden, Heaven was closed for "normal traffic" until Jesus died for us on the cross. The fall of Adam and Eve had shut Heaven's gates against us. With the possible exception of Elijah and Enoch (who are listed in the Bible as "taken up into Heaven"–Heb 11:5; 2Kgs 2:9-1) no humans had yet gone to Heaven until Jesus opened the gates and took a host of "captives" with Him. According to the Bible, no one is yet in Hell. Hell does not become operative until the Second Coming (Rev 19:20-20:3).

The despoiling of Sheol, the defeat of Satan and the opening of Heaven's gates happened in the following way. Immediately after the crucifixion, Jesus went to Sheol and awakened the souls of the righteous dead, preached the Gospel to them and took their souls to that Heaven where God dwells, the third Heaven (according to 2 Cor 12:2) not to be confused with the heavenly places where Satan and his angels dwell since they were cast out of Heaven (Eph 3:10), or the heavens in Genesis chapters one and two, which seem to refer to our outer space.

For almost 2000 years, the traditional Apostle's Creed acknowledged Jesus' visit to Sheol saying "...He was crucified, dead and buried. **He descended into Hell.** On the third day He arose again. He ascended into Heaven and sits at the right hand of the Father from which He comes to judge the living and the dead…." The word "Hell" here actually is Hades, the place of the dead, not Hell the place of eternal judgment. Because of this mistranslation based on the King James Bible, the line has been dropped from many (but not all) readings and oral presentations. Nonetheless, it has been a central doctrine of the Apostle's Creed that Jesus went to Sheol between Friday afternoon and Sunday morning to proclaim Himself to the righteous dead of the Old Testament.

> *Eph 4:8-9 Therefore it says, "When He ascended on high, He led captive a host of captives, and He gave gifts to men." (Now this expression, "He ascended," what does it mean except that He also had descended into the lower parts of the earth?)*

> *1 Peter 3:18-19 For Christ also died for sins once for all, the just for the unjust, in order that He might bring us to God, having been put to death in the flesh, but made alive in the spirit; 19 in which also He went and made proclamation to the spirits now in prison. (NAS)*

After Jesus died and went to Sheol, He preached to the righteous dead and then He defeated Satan in his own realm making a public spectacle of him. He recaptured the saints of old from Satan's grip of death, thus looting Satan's "Trophy Room." The unrighteous dead were left "sleeping" in Sheol (Hades).

> *Col 2:14-15 having canceled out the certificate of debt consisting of decrees against us and which was hostile to us; and He has taken it out of the way, having nailed it to the cross. 15 When He had disarmed the rulers and authorities, He made a public display of them, having triumphed over them through Him. (NAS)*

> *Ps 68:18-27 Thou hast ascended on high, Thou hast led captive {Thy} captives. Thou hast received gifts among men, even {among} the rebellious also, that the LORD God may dwell {there.} Blessed be the Lord, who daily bears our burden, the God {who} is our*

salvation. God is to us a God of deliverances; and to GOD the Lord belongs escape from death. Surely God will shatter the head of His enemies, the hairy crown of him who goes on in his guilty deeds. The Lord said, "I will bring {them} back from Bashan. <u>I will bring {them} back from the depths of the sea; that your foot may shatter {them} in blood, the tongue of your dogs {may have} its portion from {your} enemies." They have seen Thy procession, O God, the procession of my God, my King, into the sanctuary</u>. The singers went on, the musicians after {them} in the midst of the maidens beating tambourines. Bless God in the congregations, {even} the LORD, {you who are} of the fountain of Israel. There is Benjamin, the youngest, ruling them, the princes of Judah {in} their throng, the princes of Zebulun, the princes of Naphtali. (NAS)

Here is a detailed description of Jesus leading the Old Testament saints by tribes into the sanctuary of God. This is the "exodus" out of Sheol, the valley of death, and into heaven, itself. It is a festive celebratory event and calls to mind an enigmatic, almost humorous passage in Matthew's gospel. Apparently some of these overjoyed saints got a little carried away in the process and decided to visit some unsuspecting relatives on the way.

Matt 27:49-54 And Jesus cried out again with a loud voice, and yielded up His spirit. 51 and behold, the veil of the temple was torn in two from top to bottom, and the earth shook; and the rocks were split, 52 and the tombs were opened; and many bodies of the saints who had fallen asleep were raised; 53 and coming out of the tombs after His resurrection they entered the holy city and appeared to many. (NAS)

The end of this amazing exodus is seen in Psalm 24 when Jesus challenges and commands the gates of Heaven to open for them. These gates which had been barred against mankind since the fall of Adam are once again opened for human admittance.

Ps 24:1-10 The earth is the LORD'S, and all it contains, the world, and those who dwell in it. For He has founded it upon the seas, and established it upon the rivers. <u>Who may ascend into the hill of the</u>

LORD? And who may stand in His holy place? He who has clean hands and a pure heart, who has not lifted up his soul to falsehood, and has not sworn deceitfully. He shall receive a blessing from the LORD and righteousness from the God of his salvation. This is the generation of those who seek Him, who seek Thy face– {even} Jacob. Selah. Lift up your heads, O gates, and be lifted up, O ancient doors, that the King of glory may come in! Who is the King of glory? The LORD strong and mighty, the LORD mighty in battle. Lift up your heads, O gates, and lift {them} up, O ancient doors, that the King of glory may come in! Who is this King of glory? The LORD of hosts, He is the King of glory. Selah. (NAS)

The souls of the believers now go directly to Heaven, bypassing Sheol, because for the believer "to be absent of the body is to be present with Christ." The souls of the unrighteous continue to populate Sheol until the Great White Throne judgment, also referred to in Matthew 25 as the judgment between the sheep and the goats.

*2 Cor 5:5-10 Now He who prepared us for this very purpose is God, who gave to us the Spirit as a pledge. 6 Therefore, being always of good courage, and knowing that **while we are at home in the body we are absent from the Lord**– 7 for we walk by faith, not by sight– 8 we are of good courage, I say, and prefer rather to be absent from the body and to be at home with the Lord. 9 Therefore also we have as our ambition, whether at home or absent, to be pleasing to Him. 10 For we must all appear before the judgment seat of Christ, that each one may be recompensed for his deeds in the body, according to what he has done, whether good or bad.* (NAS)

Many believers are unaware that Psalms 22, 23 and 24 can be read as a prophetic description of this whole process. It can be seen as a poetic suite of three movements or a play with 3 acts. In Psalm 22 (as we have shown before) we get a perfect prophetic description of the Crucifixion.

Psalm 24 is a description of His ascending into heaven on Sunday morning. Remember, he told Mary the Magdalene, *"...do not touch me for I have not yet ascended to the Father"* (Jn 20:17). Yet later that same day He is inviting one and all to touch Him, to embrace

Him, etc (Jn 20:19; Lk 24:39). This ascending to the Father on Sunday is not to be confused with His Ascension into Heaven 40 days later. This ascending is for the purpose of bringing the captive saints from Sheol to the Father and demonstrating his victory to all. He has despoiled Sheol of Satan's trophies, the spoils of Satan's battle with God for the souls of men.. This is Psalm 24 and Ephesians 4:8-9 and Psalm 68:18.

But what can we see in Psalm 23, the oh-so-famous Psalm 23–The Lord is My Shepherd? It is here that we get a picture of Jesus in Sheol–the valley of the shadow of death. Even in Sheol, we are called to abide in faith, to trust the Lord to deliver us. Even in the realm of our enemies, God spreads a table before us. He anoints our heads with oil. We will fear no evil because He leads us in triumph even in Sheol. These were the images in Jesus' mind as He died on the Cross. That is why He could pray for us, *"Father, forgive them for they know not what they are doing."*

One might ask then, "Does this not constitute a second chance after death? I thought we agreed earlier that a second chance after death was not Biblical (Heb 9:27)." We DID agree to that and NO, this does not constitute a second chance. This is, in fact, their first chance to accept Jesus as their Lord and Savior, their Kinsman-Redeemer. The scripture tells us that God knows what is in a man's heart, and that God can see the end from the beginning (Is 46:9-10). God knows before we are even born who will choose Him and who will reject Him (Ps 139). God has foreknowledge (Acts 2:23; Rom 8:29; 11:2; 1Peter 1:2,20). This means that God would have known who in Sheol had a heart to receive Him.

Romans 8:28-30 tells us that he whom God foreknows will receive Him, He calls and He seals. He will *"predestine them to conform to the image of His Son."* God does the work of salvation in every person and in every age. We merely choose to obey or to rebel, to follow or to run away, to receive Him or to reject Him. The Bible shows a caring, fair and just God who will find a way to offer every man and woman in every place in every age a chance to be saved, even if my brain, my experience and my understanding cannot comprehend how He will accomplish it. Paul tells us that what can be known about God is evident in nature around us and in our hearts, our consciences bearing witness to right and wrong (Rom 1:18-23; 2:14). Therefore, he says, we are without excuse, each and every one of us (Rom 1:20; 2:1).

We are all held accountable to seek and find God. If we seek Him, we will find Him. God reveals Himself to those who seek Him, whose hearts are toward Him (2 Chron 15:1-2; Ezra 8:22; Ps 22:26; 24:6; Heb 11:6). In a world where the Bible and Biblical preaching are present and plentiful, everyone can know that salvation comes exclusively through Jesus. We are without excuse. But there are times and places where the Bible has never been revealed and the Gospel has not been preached. What do we do with those people? Do they just go to Hell because they were "unlucky" enough to have been born in such times and places? Some say that they do. They assume that God can only offer Jesus by means of books and missionaries. And yet the evidence is to the contrary.

Here in the Bible, in these verses, we see God sending Jesus to Sheol to "preach the Gospel to the spirits in prison," that is, the righteous dead in Sheol. The word "righteous" means rightly related to God, not sinless. Many people in the Bible were referred to as righteous who were obviously sinners. Lot, David, Job, and Jacob come to mind. So Jesus went to Sheol to preach to those who had been rightly related to God in their lifetime but had never had a presentation of salvation through Jesus. *Abraham believed God and it was accounted to Him as righteousness* (Gen 15:6; Rom 4:3, 9; Jas 2:23), but Abraham was not sinless. All salvation is based in relationship, not in works or rituals or doctrinal purity, according to Paul's Letter to the Romans, the Galatians, the Ephesians and others.

In the autobiography, The Heavenly Man, we read the story of Brother Yun and the leaders of the Chinese house church movement. He tells us that Jesus appeared to him and other house church founders even before he had heard there was a Jesus. Missionaries tell us stories of encountering people who were told by God that they were coming with a message of salvation. The Old Testament tells us stories about God and even Jesus Himself revealing Himself to men and women unbidden and unexpected. There are many additional stories about God or Jesus sending angels with messages of salvation on their behalf. Although we may not be able to understand all the details of these visitations, we can see enough to know God's heart and His ethical commitment to fairness and justice. Too often in order to oversimplify, we paint God as a monster, a cold-hearted unjust judge and an unfeeling creator who values doctrine more than people. The Bible, taken as a whole, would not support such an image of God.

God is on record as not wishing that anyone would be lost (2 Pet 3:9). It is in His heart to offer salvation to everyone. He knows that many will reject Him and His salvation, yet He loves everyone even before they love Him (Rom 5:8). So we know where His heart is in the matter. We can see that His plan requires us to come to Him through Jesus (Acts 4:12), and we can also see that He goes out of His way to offer Jesus to people in every age and in every place. This leads us to trust that He has a mechanism for everyone in every age and in every place to find Jesus, even if we do not know how He will accomplish that. We just need to trust Him. He will explain it to us later. The despoiling of Sheol is support for and justification of that trust.

Chapter 8

The Second Coming of the Messiah - The Tribulation and the Antichrist

THE BIBLE TELLS us that prior to the return of the Lord there will be a <u>seven-year period of Tribulation</u> upon the earth, culminating in the Second Coming of Christ. A world leader will emerge who captures the imagination of all nations. He is popularly known as the Antichrist (1 Jn 2:18; 2:22; 3:43; 2 Jn 7), but the Bible also calls him the Beast (Rev 13) and the man of lawlessness (2 Thess 2:3). He exhibits signs and wonders and has a very persuasive tongue. He convinces Israel to trust him and is thought by many Jews to be the coming Messiah. He appears to bring long sought after peace to the Middle East and the promise of worldwide tranquility. He rises to world dominance and the nations follow after him. Empowered by Satan (the Dragon), he exercises authority in both political and religious spheres and installs a religious leader to assist him. This second leader is known as the False Prophet. For three and one-half years, the Antichrist seems to be fulfilling his promises toward Israel, but in the midst of the seven-year period he breaks his covenant with Israel and brings intense persecution upon all Jews and believers. It is in response to the desperate and sincere prayers of the persecuted Jews that Jesus appears as their Messiah.

DANIEL'S TEACHING ON THE ESCHATON

Dan 9:27 "And he will make a firm covenant with the many for one week, but in the middle of the week he will put a stop to sacrifice and grain offering; and on the wing of abominations will come one who makes desolate, even until a complete destruction, one that is decreed, is poured out on the one who makes desolate." (NAS)

(For technical reasons related to the apocalyptic genre in which this was written, the "week" above means "a week of years" or seven years. Consequently, the middle of the week is three and one-half years. For a more thorough explanation of this concept, see Appendix II)

The coming of this Antichrist was predicted with specificity as far back as the Book of Daniel in chapters seven and eight. Many have been skeptical about his apocalyptic writing and its connection to the Eschaton, but among those who have supported this construct are Jesus, Paul and John the Revelator. Before we see what they had to say about Daniel's prophecies, let us first understand Daniel. In the first year of Belshazzar's reign (553 B.C.), Daniel had a vision about four beasts. Daniel provided the historical explanation for these beasts in chapters two and seven of his prophetic book. The first three beasts are Babylon, Media/Persia and Greece. The fourth beast represents the physical Roman Empire and its spiritual successor, the one-world government of the Eschaton. Jesus evokes Daniel's images in His end-time explanations as does John in the Book of Revelation. In fact, Jesus often refers to Himself as the Son of Man, a Messianic term born in Daniel 7:13.

Dan 7:1-6 In the first year of Belshazzar king of Babylon, Daniel saw a dream and visions in his mind as he lay on his bed; then he wrote the dream down and related the following summary of it. 2 Daniel said, "I was looking in my vision by night, and behold, the four winds of heaven were stirring up the great sea. 3 "And four great beasts were coming up from the sea, different from one another. 4 "The first was like a lion and had the wings of an eagle (Babylon Ez 1:1-14). I kept looking until its wings were plucked, and it was lifted up from the ground and made to stand on two feet like a man; a human mind also was given to it. 5 "And behold, another beast, a second one, resembling a bear. (Medea/Persia) And it was raised up on one side, and three ribs were in its mouth between its teeth; and thus they said to it, 'Arise, devour much

meat!' 6 "After this I kept looking, and behold, another one, like a leopard, (Greece) which had on its back four wings of a bird; the beast also had four heads, and dominion was given to it. (NAS)
(Alexander and his four generals–Lysimachus, Ptolemy, Seleucus and Cassander)

In Revelation 13:1-5, the beast (Antichrist) is seen as a composite of all three of the creatures in Daniel's vision. They were all ruthless world conquerors. This composite beast is empowered by the dragon, who is clearly identified later as Satan. The Antichrist shares with these despots in Daniel the same nature and the same mentor or driving force, Satan. Like them, he operates in a spirit of conquest, devastation, control and death. Like them, he is attempting to take over the world.

Rev 13:1-5 And he stood on the sand of the seashore. And I saw a beast coming up out of the sea, having ten horns and seven heads, and on his horns were ten diadems, and on his heads were blasphemous names. 2 And the beast which I saw was like a <u>leopard</u>, and his feet were like those of a <u>bear</u>, and his mouth like the mouth of a <u>lion</u>. And the dragon gave him his power and his throne and great authority. 3 And I saw one of his heads as if it had been slain, and his fatal wound was healed. And the whole earth was amazed and followed after the beast; 4 and they worshiped the dragon, because he gave his authority to the beast; and they worshiped the beast, saying, "Who is like the beast, and who is able to wage war with him?" (NAS)

Dan 7:7 "After this I kept looking in the night visions, and behold, a fourth beast, dreadful and terrifying and extremely strong; and it had large iron teeth. It devoured and crushed, and trampled down the remainder with its feet; and it was different from all the beasts that were before it, and it had ten horns. 8 "While I was contemplating the horns, behold, another horn, a little one, came up among them, and three of the first horns were pulled out by the roots before it; and behold, this horn possessed eyes like the eyes of a man, and a mouth uttering great boasts. (Rev 13: 5-6; 2 Thess 2:1-4)

Here in Daniel we see a fourth beast, the one with the ten horns. This is the Roman Empire which is historically the fourth great ruthless world conqueror of Daniel's prophecy that is featured prominently in Daniel 11. The Antichrist in Rev 13 above is also identified with this beast. He emerges from out of the people of the ten horns, is empowered by the same spirit and comes with the same mandate; i.e., world domination and hostility towards God's people. This is more fully described later on in Dan 7:19-25 (see below).

Dan 7:9 "I kept looking Until thrones were set up, (Rev 1:4; 3:21; 4:2-10; 5: 1-13; 6:16; 7:9-17; 8:3; 12:5; 20:11-12 GWT) and the Ancient of Days took His sea. His vesture was like white snow, and the hair of His head like pure wool (Rev 1:14). His throne was ablaze with flames, its wheels were a burning fire (Rev 4:2-5). 10 "A river of fire was flowing and coming out from before Him. Thousands upon thousands were attending Him, and myriads upon myriads were standing before Him (Rev 5:11-14; Heb 12:22). The court sat, and the books were opened. (Rev 5:1-10; 10:1-11); (Rev 3:5; 13:8; 17:8; 20:12-15)

It is clear here that Daniel is seeing the same place and players as did John in the book of Revelation and the same throne as in Ezekiel chapters one and ten. Solomon had the temple decorated with these same images (1Kgs 7). This is the throne of God and account books are about to be read. This speaks of judgment.

Dan 7:11 "Then I kept looking because of the sound of the boastful words which the horn was speaking; (Rev 13:5-6; 2 Thess 2:1-4) I kept looking until the beast was slain, and its body was destroyed and given to the burning fire. (Rev 19:20; 20:14-15; 21:8) 12 "As for the rest of the beasts, their dominion was taken away, but an extension of life was granted to them for an appointed period of time. 13 "I kept looking in the night visions, and behold, with the clouds of heaven One like a Son of Man was coming (Rev 1:7; Mt 24:30; 26:64; 1 Thess 4:17), and He came up to the Ancient of Days and was presented before Him. 14 "And to Him was given dominion, glory and a kingdom, that all the peoples, nations, and men of every language might serve Him. His dominion is an everlasting

dominion which will not pass away; and His kingdom is one which
will not be destroyed. (Rev 1: 6; 5:13; 11:15)

Daniel is witnessing the ultimate destruction of the Beast (the Antichrist) and all other despots (*the rest of the beasts*). Daniel also sees the establishment of Jesus on the throne as the conqueror of all things. He (Jesus) is given final dominion in the earth and for all eternity for His victory over the Beast. The reign of Jesus in this dimension and magnitude has not happened yet. This is an event that must occur after the Second Coming. Daniel is seeing into the Eschaton. There is more on this in Daniel 7:26-27 and Daniel 8:22-26 below.

Dan 7:15 "As for me, Daniel, my spirit was distressed within me, and the visions in my mind kept alarming me. 16 "I approached one of those who were standing by and began asking him the exact meaning of all this. So he told me and made known to me the interpretation of these things: 17 'These great beasts, which are four in number, are four kings who will arise from the earth. 18 'But the saints of the Highest One will receive the kingdom and possess the kingdom forever, for all ages to come.' (Rev 5:9; 1:6)

Daniel seeks and is given an explanation that has both near-term and end-time implications and meaning.

Dan 7:19 "Then I desired to know the exact meaning of the fourth beast, which was different from all the others, exceedingly dreadful, with its teeth of iron and its claws of bronze, and which devoured, crushed, and trampled down the remainder with its feet, 20 and the meaning of the ten horns that were on its head, and the other horn which came up, and before which three of them fell, namely, that horn which had eyes and a mouth uttering great boasts, and which was larger in appearance than its associates. (Rev 12;3; 13:1-3; 17:3-16) 21 "I kept looking, and that horn was waging war with the saints and overpowering them 22 until the Ancient of Days came (Rev 11:7; 12:7-17; 13:7; 17:12-15), and judgment was passed in favor of the saints of the Highest One, and the time arrived when the saints took possession of the kingdom. 23 "Thus he said: 'The fourth beast will be a fourth kingdom on the earth, which will be different from all the other kingdoms, and it will devour the whole earth and tread it down and crush it. 24 'As for the ten horns, out of this kingdom ten kings will arise; and another will arise after them, and he will be different from the previous ones and will subdue three kings. 25 'And he will speak out against the Most High and wear down the saints of the Highest One, and he will intend to make alterations in times and in law; and they will be given into his hand for a time, times, and half a time. (Rev 12:14; 11:2; 12:6; 13:5; Dan 9:27; 12:11)

Daniel is told that the fourth beast is larger in scope and more evil than the other three. In his day, he will wage war on God's people and blaspheme God Himself. He will have supreme power so as to change the way of reckoning time and to change the law globally. He will have success in this for three and one-half years (See Appendix II).

Dan 7:26 'But the court will sit for judgment, (Rev 20:10-15) and his dominion will be taken away, annihilated and destroyed forever. 27 'Then the sovereignty, the dominion, and the greatness of all the kingdoms under the whole heaven will be given to the people of the saints of the Highest One; His kingdom will be an everlasting kingdom, and all the dominions will serve and obey Him.' (NAS)

Daniel is given a vision of the demise and judgment of the Beast, the victory of God's people and the establishment of an everlasting kingdom in which his people, Israel, play a prominent role. This is revealed to him because of his ever-present concern for the well-being of his exiled countrymen. Daniel is always asking God what is going to happen to Israel. (This concern finally results in Daniel's bold and impassioned prayer in Daniel 9:1-23 that leads to the extraordinary revelation of "the seventy weeks of Daniel.")

Dan 8:22-26 "And the broken horn and the four horns that arose in its place represent four kingdoms which will arise from his nation, although not with his power. 23 "And in the latter period of their rule, when the transgressors have run their course, a king will arise insolent and skilled in intrigue. 24 "And his power will be mighty, but not by his own power, and he will destroy to an extraordinary degree and prosper and perform his will; he will destroy mighty men and the holy people. 25 "And through his shrewdness He will cause deceit to succeed by his influence; and he will magnify himself in his heart, and he will destroy many while they are at ease. He will even oppose the Prince of princes, but he will be broken without human agency. (Rev 20:1-3) 26 "And the vision of the evenings and mornings which has been told is true; but keep the vision secret, for it pertains to many days in the future." (NAS)

In Daniel 8, in yet another vision, Daniel is given much of the same information about he rise and fall of the Antichrist, his deceptive and destructive ways, his hostility toward God's people and his personal empowerment by Satan. Daniel is also told that this part of the vision is futuristic, not for Daniel's day. Daniel 11 tells us that this type of spiritually empowered evil despot arose in about 170B.C. and made war on God's people. His name was Antiochus Epiphanes. It is to him that Jesus points as an example or "metaphorical type" of the Antichrist who was yet to come. Jesus is pointing to the Eschaton.

JESUS' TEACHING ON THE ESCHATON

More important to us than the coordination between Daniel and Revelation are **the words of Jesus Himself** as recorded in Matthew, Mark and Luke in their Gospels.

Matt 24:3-31 And as (Jesus) was sitting on the Mount of Olives, the disciples came to Him privately, saying, "Tell us, when will these things be, and what will be the sign of Your coming, and of the end of the age?"

Jesus is asked about the Second Coming and about the end of time–the Eschaton.

Matt 24:4 And Jesus answered and said to them, "See to it that no one misleads you. 5 "For many will come in My name, saying, 'I am the Christ,' and will mislead many. 6 "And you will be hearing of wars and rumors of wars; see that you are not frightened, for *those things must take place, but <u>that is not yet the end.</u> 7 "For nation will rise against nation, and kingdom against kingdom, and in various places there will be famines and earthquakes. 8 "But all these things are merely the beginning of birth pangs. 9 "<u>Then they will deliver you</u> **to tribulation**, and will kill you, and you will be hated by all nations on account of My name (Dan 7:20-25). 10 "And at that time many will fall away and will deliver up one another and hate one another. 11 "And many false prophets will arise, and will mislead many. 12 "And because lawlessness is increased, most people's love will grow cold. 13 "But the one who endures to the end, he shall be saved. 14 "And this gospel of the kingdom shall be preached in the whole world for a witness to all the nations, and then the end shall come.*

Jesus tells them that it will be many days off into the future and many things must happen first. There will be many famines, wars, earthquakes of the "garden variety" which are just the beginning of it all. They are metaphorical types of the final events. There will be apostasy, betrayal, false prophets, genocide, lawlessness and a worldwide diminishment of people's devotion for God. Jesus tells them (and us) that we must endure tribulation to be saved. This was a constant theme in Jesus' teachings–endurance results in salvation. It is the theme of both the book of Hebrews and the book of Revelation. It is a theme in Paul's writings as well. Nowhere is there even an inkling of a promise of a divine rescue mission. Jesus tells us, *"In the world you have tribulation, but take courage; I have overcome the world."* (John 16:33 (NAS)). Our job is to preach the gospel to all nations. After that has been accomplished, the end will come.

Matt 24:15 "Therefore when you see the abomination of desolation which was spoken of through Daniel the prophet, standing in the holy place (let the reader understand), (Dan 9:27; 12:11; 11:31) 16 then let those who are in Judea flee to the mountains; 17 let him who is on the housetop not go down to get the things out that are in his house; 18 and let him who is in the field not turn back to get his cloak. 19 "But woe to those who are with child and to those who nurse babes in those days! 20 "But pray that your flight may not be in the winter, or on a Sabbath; 21 for <u>then there will be a</u>

great tribulation, such as has not occurred since the beginning of
the world until now, nor ever shall. 22 "And unless those days had
been cut short, no life would have been saved; but for the sake of
the elect those days shall be cut short.

Jesus tells us plainly that the Great Tribulation "...*such as has*
not occurred since the beginning of the world until now, nor ever
shall.." will be preceded by the Abomination of Desolation spoken
of by Daniel.

What is the Abomination of Desolation spoken of by Daniel? An
all-powerful ruler sets up a statue in the Holy of Holies and requires
worship of it from God's people. History records and Daniel 11 and
12 predict that the Seleucid (Syrian) king, Antiochus IV would attempt
to stomp out religious Judaism in favor of Greek Hellenism. On
December 25, 167B.C., after much frustration he forcibly conquered
Jerusalem, set a statue of Zeus in the Holy of Holies and sacrificed
hogs to it. His actions leading up to this provoked the family of an
orthodox priest (the Maccabees) to rise up militarily and, over time
through guerilla warfare, drive him out. During that time, the temple
worship ceased for 1150 days and nights (see also Dan 8:14). When
he was dislodged and the temple was cleansed and rededicated on
December 25, 164B.C., God worked a miracle that allowed a single
store of anointed oil to miraculously last for eight days until some
more could be produced. That is the genesis of the Jewish Feast
of Lights or Hanukkah. All Jews were and are very familiar with
this story. Jesus points backwards to it and says when they witness
that same desolation again in the future, they will know that the
Eschaton has arrived. That is what He means by the Abomination
of Desolation.

Matt 24:23 "Then if anyone says to you, 'Behold, here is the Christ,'
or 'There He is,' do not believe him. 24 "For false Christs and
*false prophets will arise and will show great signs and wonders, **so***
***as to mislead, if possible, even the elect**. 25 "Behold, I have told*
you in advance. 26 "If therefore they say to you, 'Behold, He is
in the wilderness,' do not go forth, or, 'Behold, He is in the inner
rooms,' do not believe them. 27 "For just as the lightning comes

from the east, and flashes even to the west, so shall the coming of the Son of Man be. 28 "Wherever the corpse is, there the vultures will gather.

Jesus warns them (and us) that false prophets and false Christs will come and some will even be able to work signs and wonders. If we are not attuned to the voice of God, and we do not know our Bible, **even the elect can be fooled**. Jesus assures them (and us) that every eye will see His return. In the same way that lightning fills up the sky and all see it and in the way that vultures circle over the carrion and all know that something is dead, everyone will see His return. It will not be in secret.

Matt 24:29 "But immediately after the tribulation of those days the sun will be darkened, and the moon will not give its light, and the stars will fall from the sky, and the powers of the heavens will be shaken, 30 and then the sign of the Son of Man will appear in the sky, and then all the tribes of the earth will mourn, and they will see the Son of Man coming on the clouds of the sky with power and great glory. 31 "And He will send forth His angels <u>with a great trumpet</u> and they <u>will gather together His elect</u> from from the four winds, from one end of the sky to the other. (NAS)

The Second Coming will be marked by significant geological upheaval and signs in the heavens. This leads one to think of meteor showers or comets. At that time, there will be a gathering of all believers, an event sometimes known as the rapture of the church. Notice that it is timed to occur at the Second Coming, an event that occurs at or near the end of the Great Tribulation. (More on that to follow.)

2 Thess 2:1-12 Now we request you, brethren, with regard to the coming of our Lord Jesus Christ, and our gathering together to Him, 2 that you may not be quickly shaken from your composure or be disturbed either by a spirit or a message or a letter as if from us, to the effect that the day of the Lord has come. 3 Let no one in any way deceive you, for it will not come unless the apostasy comes

first, and the man of lawlessness is revealed, the son of destruction,
4 who opposes and exalts himself above every so-called god or
object of worship, so that he takes his seat in the temple of God,
displaying himself as being God. 5 Do you not remember that while
I was still with you, I was telling you these things?

Paul has a similar conversation with his followers about the Second Coming and other eschatological events. He speaks about widespread apostasy, the emergence of the Antichrist, the Abomination of Desolation. He reminds them that they have heard this teaching before.

6 And you know what restrains him now, so that in his time he may
be revealed. 7 For the mystery of lawlessness is already at work;
only he who now restrains will do so until he is taken out of the
way. 8 And then that lawless one will be revealed whom the Lord
will slay with the breath of His mouth and bring to an end by the
appearance of His coming; 9 that is, the one whose coming is in
accord with the activity of Satan, with all power and signs and false
wonders, 10 and with all the deception of wickedness for those
who perish, because they did not receive the love of the truth so
as to be saved. 11 And for this reason God will send upon them a
deluding influence so that they might believe what is false, 12 in
order that they all may be judged who did not believe the truth, but
took pleasure in wickedness. (NAS)

Paul tells them that the spirit of the Antichrist works in every age and will be restrained until it is the right time in history for him to be revealed. That which restrains him now is God's Spirit. God is in control and will not let the events of the Eschaton unfold until all of the foreknown ones have come to the Lord (see 2 Pet 3:8-11 below). People who love and obey God need not fear the Second Coming of Christ. However, those whose hearts are at enmity with God and His Christ will be allowed to believe what they wish to believe, even to their own destruction, because they took delight in opposing God.

PETER'S TEACHING ON THE ESCHATON

Peter supports and reiterates the teachings of Jesus and Paul concerning the events of the Eschaton and offers even more insight and advice. He tells us that people will scoff at the idea of a Second Coming.

2 Peter 3:2-5 Know this first of all, that in the last days mockers will come with their mocking, following after their own lusts, 4 and saying, "Where is the promise of His coming? For ever since the fathers fell asleep, all continues just as it was from the beginning of creation." (NAS)

In his discussion of the Eschaton, he reaffirms his belief in the Genesis accounts of creation and Noah's flood and then tells us that, in the end, the earth will be destroyed by fire in a "day reserved for the destruction of evil men." He believes that God has an "exit plan."

5 For when they maintain this, it escapes their notice that by the word of God the heavens existed long ago and the earth was formed out of water and by water, 6 through which the world at that time was destroyed, being flooded with water. 7 But the present heavens and earth by His word are being reserved for fire, kept for the day of judgment and destruction of ungodly men. (NAS)

He tells us that while it may seem like a long time for the fulfillment of these prophecies (and yet nothing has happened), God thinks of 1,000 years in the same way we think of one day. In that light, as far as God is concerned, it has been just a little over a week since creation. God is not late. And He is not impotent. He can and will perform His will in the earth. In His great love for mankind, God is just patient so that as many as possible may be saved. While we may long for the Second Coming, we are glad that He waited until after we were born, or we would have missed Heaven altogether.

2 Peter 3:8-11 But do not let this one fact escape your notice, beloved, that with the Lord one day is as a thousand years, and a thousand years as one day. 9 The Lord is not slow about His promise, as some count slowness, but is patient toward you, not wishing for any to perish but for all to come to repentance. (NAS)

Peter goes on to tell us that when it happens, it will happen suddenly and unexpectedly for most people. He reveals that although God will destroy the present heavens and scorch the earth by fire, He will immediately create a new heaven and a new earth to be inhabited by mankind

2 Peter 3:10-13 But the day of the Lord will come like a thief, in which the heavens will pass away with a roar and the elements will be destroyed with intense heat, and the earth and its works will be burned up. 11 Since all these things are to be destroyed in this way, what sort of people ought you to be in holy conduct and godliness, 12 looking for and hastening the coming of the day of God, on account of which the heavens will be destroyed by burning, and the elements will melt with intense heat! 13 But according to His promise we are looking for new heavens and a new earth, in which righteousness dwells. (NAS)

In Acts 2:19-22, Peter had told the multitudes who heard him preach at Pentecost that in the last days God would cleanse the earth by fire. In doing so, he was quoting the prophet Joel 2:28-32. In Matthew 24:21, Jesus is Himself quoting Joel 2:2. Sodom and Gomorrah were destroyed by fire that fell from the heavens. All Jews knew this story. Moses called down fire from the sky upon Egypt. Everywhere in the Scriptures fire is used as a symbol for purification. The writings of the prophets are replete with metaphors of fire consuming the evil arrayed against God and against His people. The connection between the purging fire of God and the coming of the Lord is solid throughout the Scriptures.

Acts 2:19-22 'And I will grant wonders in the sky above, and signs on the earth beneath, blood, and fire, and vapor of smoke. 20 'The sun shall be turned into darkness, and the moon into blood, before the great and glorious day of the Lord shall come. 21 'And it shall be, that everyone who calls on the name of the Lord shall be saved.' (NAS)

Finally, Peter finishes by telling his flock that the soon coming of the Lord should be used as a motivator to good works and a warning to be on guard against false teachers. He tells them they should particularly pay attention to Paul (who, interestingly enough he admits, is sometimes hard to understand) (2 Peter 3:14-18).

2 Peter 3:14-18 Therefore, beloved, since you look for these things, be diligent to be found by Him in peace, spotless and blameless, 15 and regard the patience of our Lord to be salvation; just as also our beloved brother Paul, according to the wisdom given him, wrote to you, 16 as also in all his letters, speaking in them of these things, in which are some things hard to understand, which the untaught and unstable distort, as they do also the rest of the Scriptures, to their own destruction. 17 You therefore, beloved, knowing this beforehand, be on your guard lest, being carried away by the error of unprincipled men, you fall from your own steadfastness, 18 but grow in the grace and knowledge of our Lord and Savior Jesus Christ. To Him be the glory, both now and to the day of eternity. Amen. (NAS)

JOHN'S TEACHING ON THE ESCHATON

John reiterates much of what the others have already said. His book of Revelation is a study in its own right, but he adds an interesting point that flows from the fact that he lived longer than all of the others and, therefore, witnessed more over time. He tells us that Antichrists have gone out "from among us." The spirit of Antichrist resides in many down through the ages and can arise from within the church as well. They are false teachers who with persuasive words lead God's people to destruction. In our own day they are sometimes pastors, teachers and even seminary professors who twist the Scriptures and manipulate God's own word against the Kingdom of Heaven. Even Satan quotes scripture (Mt 4:6). There is a place reserved in the Lake of Fire for such as these. We must not be fooled by "modern enlightenment" that seeks to undermine the time-honored Word of God in our day.

1 John 2:18-19 Children, it is the last hour; and just as you heard that antichrist is coming, even now many Antichrists have arisen; from this we know that it is the last hour. 19 They went out from us, but they were not really of us; for if they had been of us, they would have remained with us; but they went out, in order that it might be shown that they all are not of us. (NAS)

Chapter 9

The Second Coming - The Timing and the Parable of the Fig Tree

NOT MUCH IS known about the timing of the Second Coming. Jesus said that He Himself did not know the timing of His own return. Only the Father in Heaven knows. Down through the ages, men have claimed to be able to predict it, but they have always been wrong. Many people have lost fortunes, families and their faith trying to guess God's plan and God's timing. It is a fool's errand. So we are not going to claim to know either.

Jesus tells us that we have enough information to understand what is going on as it unfolds, if we have "eyes that can see and ears that can hear." We will need to be rightly related to God and schooled in His Word in order to recognize the signs of His coming.

SIGNS OF HIS COMING

The ultimate timing of the Second Coming according to Jesus is associated with the "**ripening of the fig tree**." Since the fig tree is a Biblical symbol for Israel (Hos 9:10; Joel 1:6-7), many have taken this as a reference to the 1948 restoration of Israel as a nation in Palestine. The promise is often interpreted to mean that the generation that witnesses this event (the ripening of the fig tree) will not all pass away before the Second Coming of the Lord. If true, this would mean that those born as of 1948 (the baby boomers) will not have all died before the Second Coming.

Luke 13:6-9 And He began telling this parable: "A certain man had a fig tree which had been planted in his vineyard; and he came looking for fruit on it, and did not find any. 7 "And he said to the vineyard-keeper, 'Behold, <u>for three years I have come looking for fruit on this fig tree without finding any</u>. Cut it down! Why does it even use up the ground?' 8 "And he answered and said to him, 'Let it alone, sir, for this year too, until I dig around it and put in fertilizer; 9 and if it bears fruit next year, fine; but if not, cut it down.' (NAS)

Matt 24:32-44 "Now learn <u>the parable from the fig tree</u>: when its branch has already become tender, and puts forth its leaves, you know that summer is near; 33 even so you too, when you see all these things, recognize that He is near, right at the door. 34 "Truly I say to you, this generation will not pass away until all these things take place. 35 "Heaven and earth will pass away, but My words shall not pass away. 36 "<u>But of that day and hour no one knows, not even the angels of heaven, nor the Son, but the Father alone.</u> 37 "For the coming of the Son of Man will be just like the days of Noah. 38 "For as in those days which were before the flood they were eating and drinking, they were marrying and giving in marriage, until the day that Noah entered the ark, 39 and they did not understand until the flood came and took them all away; so shall the coming of the Son of Man be.

THE SUDDENNESS OF HIS APPEARANCE

One thing is for sure. No one will miss the actual event. It will be as subtle as a lightning bolt, a meteorite, a runaway comet. Everyone knows that something is dead when they see the vultures circling. So also will everyone recognize the Coming of the Lord.

Matt 24:23-31 "Then if anyone says to you, 'Behold, here is the Christ,' or 'There He is,' do not believe him. 24 "For false Christs and false prophets will arise and will show great signs and wonders, so as to mislead, if possible, even the elect. 25 "Behold, I have told you in advance. 26 "If therefore they say to you, 'Behold, He is in the wilderness,' do not go forth, or, 'Behold, He is in the inner rooms,' do not believe them. 27 "<u>For just as the lightning comes</u>

from the east, and flashes even to the west, so shall the coming of
the Son of Man be. 28 "Wherever the corpse is, there the vultures
will gather. (NAS)

Another undeniable sign of the Second Coming is the sudden
taking away or catching up of the true believer from the earth.

Matt 24:40 "Then there shall be two men in the field; one will be
taken, and one will be left. 41 "Two women will be grinding at the
mill; one will be taken, and one will be left. 42 "Therefore be on
the alert, for you do not know which day your Lord is coming.

The events represented in Mt 24:40-42 above will occur at the
Second Coming of Christ and are often referred to as the Rapture,
even though some think they only refer to the end time purging
of the church. In either case and in spite of popular fiction to the
contrary, the Rapture occurs at the end of the seven-year period of
the Tribulation but before the wrath of God. It occurs at the Second
Coming of Jesus. (1 Cor 15:23). The rapture will come upon mankind
before many are aware that it is happening. Therefore, we must at all
time be prepared for Jesus' return. Jesus said He would come like a
thief in the night. He carries that same metaphor into His comments
in Matthew 24:43.

43 "But be sure of this, that if the head of the house had known at
what time of the night the thief was coming, he would have been
on the alert and would not have allowed his house to be broken
into. 44 "For this reason you be ready too; for the Son of Man is
coming at an hour when you do not think He will. (NAS)

Paul also uses the metaphor of the *"thief in the night"* to describe
the suddenness of Jesus' return.

1 Thess 5:1-11 Now as to the times and the epochs, brethren, you
have no need of anything to be written to you. 2 For you yourselves
know full well that the day of the Lord will come just like a thief
in the night. 3 While they are saying, "Peace and safety!" then
destruction will come upon them suddenly like birth pangs upon a
woman with child; and they shall not escape. 4 But you, brethren,

are not in darkness, that the day should overtake you like a thief;
5 for you are all sons of light and sons of day.

Paul told the Thessalonians that they needed to always be on the alert expecting the soon return of Christ. In telling them, he was also telling us to be sober, alert and living as if it could happen tomorrow. There is an inbuilt motivation in the vagueness of it. Probably it is intentional, the wisdom of a God that knows our needs.

1 Thess 5:5 We are not of night nor of darkness; 6 so then let us
not sleep as others do, but let us be alert and sober. 7 For those
who sleep do their sleeping at night, and those who get drunk get
drunk at night. 8 But since we are of the day, let us be sober, having
put on the breastplate of faith and love, and as a helmet, the hope
of salvation.

THE PURGING OF THE END TIME CHURCH

Paul also encourages us that we are not destined for God's wrath. We will have to endure the Tribulation, but only God's enemies will suffer His wrath. (More on that later.) However, there will be a significant purging of the church just preceding the return of Christ (see the Rapture of the Believers section presented later). Tribulation has a way of "separating the men from the boys."

1 Thess 5:9 For God has not destined us for wrath, but for obtaining
salvation through our Lord Jesus Christ, 10 who died for us, that
whether we are awake (alive) or asleep (dead), we may live together
with Him. 11 Therefore encourage one another, and build up one
another, just as you also are doing. (NAS)

The Israelites of Jesus' day were living in expectation of the soon coming of the Messiah and the Day of the Lord associated with it. It would be a day when Israel would be saved from its enemies. They were so focused on the Day of the Lord being a time of rescue that they did not focus on it also being a time of restoration of their relationship with God, of purging and cleansing. Malachi, the last prophet of the Old Testament, had warned them about the nature of the First Coming, but they had ignored him. His words were the last thing God said to them through the prophets until, four hundred years later, John the Baptist came out of the wilderness to preach repentance in fulfillment of Malachi's prophecy.

> *Mal 3:1-5 "Behold, I am going* to send My messenger *(**John the Baptist**), and he will clear the way before Me. And the Lord, whom you seek, will suddenly come to His temple; and the messenger of the covenant, in whom you delight, behold, He is coming," says the LORD of hosts. 2* ***"But who can endure the day of His coming? And who can stand when He appears? For He is like a refiner's fire and like fullers' soap. 3 "And He will sit as a smelter and purifier of silver, and He will purify the sons of Levi and refine them like gold and silver, so that they may present to the LORD offerings in righteousness****. 4 "Then the offering of Judah and Jerusalem will be pleasing to the LORD, as in the days of old and as in former years. 5 "Then I will draw near to you for judgment; and I will be a swift witness against the sorcerers and against the adulterers and against those who swear falsely, and against those who oppress the wage earner in his wages, the widow and the orphan, and those who turn aside the alien, and do not fear Me," says the LORD of hosts. (NAS)*

The Jews of Jesus' day missed the First Coming because they were focusing on the Second Coming. The coming of the Messiah was first and foremost a Jewish event. It had been on their hearts, in their writings and in their music since Moses' day. So when Peter gets up in the power of the Holy Spirit on Pentecost Sunday, he defines the events that occurred between the Crucifixion and the mighty wind of Pentecost as the opening salvo of the Day of the Lord and the coming of the Messiah. In Acts 2:17-21 he quotes from the prophet, Joel, saying:

> *Acts 2:17-21 'And it shall be in the last days,' God says, 'That I will pour forth of My Spirit upon all mankind; and your sons and your daughters shall prophesy, and your young men shall see visions, and your old men shall dream dreams; 18 even upon My bondslaves, both men and women, I will in those days pour forth of My Spirit and they shall prophesy. 19 'And I will grant wonders in the sky above, and signs on the earth beneath, blood, and fire,*

and vapor of smoke. 20 'The sun shall be turned into darkness, and the moon into blood, before the great and glorious day of the Lord shall come. 21 'And it shall be, that everyone who calls on the name of the Lord shall be saved.' (NAS)

God will pour out His Spirit on mankind, and YOUR sons and YOUR daughters shall prophesy and YOUR old men shall dream dreams. Israel had, and still has, a key role in the Day of the Lord and the coming of the Messiah. In a sense it is largely about Israel. All of the original Christian leaders were Jewish. Christianity was and is defined in Jewish terms. As Gentile Christians, we grow up thinking that Abraham, Isaac, Jacob, Samuel, David, Isaiah; et. al., are our ancestors and that their stories are our stories. It takes many years for some people to realize that our Old Testament is a Jewish Bible and that we Gentiles are adopted children (Rom 8:15; 9:4; Gal 4:5; Eph 1:5).

THE END TIME FOCUS ON ISRAEL

The First Coming occurred in Israel. The Second Coming will as well. Jesus was born in a Jewish village and died in a Jewish city. Even when He occasionally traveled outside of Jewish boundaries, he only addressed the Jews. Once when He was in Tyre, a Gentile city on the coast of the Mediterranean Sea, a Phoenician woman of Syrian descent, a Canaanite and a Gentile, begged Him to cast a demon out of her daughter. Jesus told her plainly that He was called only to minister to Israel. (Others would go to the Gentiles later.) He bluntly told her that it was not right to give the children's meat to the dogs. Strong words! (The story is told in Mark 7:24-30 below.)

As we discussed in the section on the Syrophoenician woman's daughter, "dogs" was an age-old euphemism among the Jews for "Gentiles." It was commonly used but it was not, as you can imagine, flattering. It was a term with a history in Israel. Even David used it in Psalm 22 to describe the Gentiles who would be at the feet of the Messiah's cross. In verse 27, Jesus calls His message "the children's bread," food meant at this time for Israel. Undeterred and full of faith, she accepts the insult and turns it on Jesus. *"Even the dogs get to eat*

the crumbs that fall from the table," she says. She acknowledges that
Jesus' ministry and miracles are for the Jews, but asks merely for the
"spillage." Jesus was amazed at her faith and granted her wish. He
made an exception for her, but Jesus was called first and foremost
to the Jews.

> *Mark 7:24-30 And from there He arose and went away to the region
> of Tyre. And when He had entered a house, <u>He wanted no one to
> know of</u> it; yet He could not escape notice. 25 But after hearing
> of Him, a woman whose little daughter had an unclean spirit,
> immediately came and fell at His feet. 26 Now the woman was a
> Gentile, of the Syrophoenician race. And she kept asking Him to
> cast the demon out of her daughter. 27 And He was saying to her,
> "Let the children be satisfied first, <u>for it is not good to take the
> children's bread and throw it to the dogs.</u>" 28 But she answered
> and said to Him, "Yes, Lord, but even the dogs under the table feed
> on the children's crumbs." 29 And He said to her, "Because of this
> answer go your way; the demon has gone out of your daughter."
> 30 And going back to her home, she found the child lying on the
> bed, the demon having departed. (NAS)*

PETER, APOSTLE TO THE CIRCUMCISED (ISRAEL)

The ministry of Peter, the Apostle, was focused on the Jews.
He became known as "an apostle to the circumcised" (Gal 2:9). At
the Last Supper, Jesus prophesied that Peter would deny Him. Then
he told Peter that once he had repented, he should *"strengthen his
brothers."* After Peter had betrayed the Lord and after the resurrection, Peter left the rest of the group and "went fishing" (John 21:3).
This means he returned to his old trade. He did not consider himself
worthy to be a minister of the Gospel. Jesus came and very pointedly
restored him to ministry and told him to "Shepherd my sheep!" (John
21:15-17). One can make the case that both "your brethren" and "My
sheep," while having broader application, can be seen as meaning
"the Jews."

Peter responded by taking on every dirty job no one else wanted.
He went to Samaria to examine a revival that had broken out there,

making a way for Samaritan Christians to be accepted among their more traditional Jewish "cousins." He went to Antioch to check on the ministry in the new controversial Gentile church. He eventually went to Rome to pastor the church in its greatest hour of persecution. He was especially beloved in the Jewish Christian groups that were outside of Israel proper.

> *1 Peter 1:1-2 Peter, an apostle of Jesus Christ, to those who reside as aliens, scattered throughout Pontus, Galatia, Cappadocia, Asia, and Bithynia, who are chosen 2 according to the foreknowledge of God the Father, by the sanctifying work of the Spirit, that you may obey Jesus Christ and be sprinkled with His blood: May grace and peace be yours in fullest measure. (NAS)*

Here in the opening lines of 1 Peter, he writes *"to those who reside as aliens, scattered throughout Pontus, Galatia, Cappadocia, Asia, and Bithynia, who are chosen."* Only Jews would be considered "aliens" by Peter in these Gentile regions. This is addressed to the Jews of the "Diaspora'–those Jews who are dispersed throughout the world. These are the same people who heard Peter preach under the anointing at Pentecost (see Acts 2:7-10). More than anyone else, Peter was the voice of Christianity to the Jews outside of Jerusalem.

He went to Cornelius' Gentile home in Caesarea and witnessed the infilling of the Holy Spirit among the Gentiles. His credentials among the Jewish Christians were so strong that when he testified about what God had done through him in the house of Cornelius, the Gentile Centurion, the elders reluctantly accepted Paul's ministry to the Gentiles as valid. Peter's word was golden among them. So when false teachers came in among them and, among other things, scorned the notion of the Second Coming or taught that it had already occurred, it was Peter who wrote to correct their understanding.

> *2 Peter 3:3 Know this first of all, that **in the last days, mockers will come with their mocking, following after their own lusts, 4 and saying, "Where is the promise of His coming**? For ever since the fathers fell asleep, all continues just as it was from the beginning of creation." 5 For when they maintain this, it escapes their notice*

*that by the word of God the heavens existed long ago and the earth
was formed out of water and by water, 6 through which the world
at that time was destroyed, being flooded with water. 7 But <u>the
present heavens and earth by His word are being reserved for fire</u>,
kept for the day of judgment* **(The Great White Throne Judgment)**
and destruction of ungodly men.

*2 Peter 3:8 But do not let this one fact escape your notice, beloved,
that with the Lord one day is as a thousand years, and a thousand
years as one day. 9 The Lord is not slow about His promise, as some
count slowness, but is patient toward you, not wishing for any to
perish but for all to come to repentance. 10 <u>But the day of the Lord
will come like a thief, in which the heavens will pass away with a
roar and the elements will be destroyed with intense heat, and the
earth and its works will be burned up</u>. 11 Since all these things
are to be destroyed in this way, what sort of people ought you to
be in holy conduct and godliness, 12 looking for and hastening the
coming of the day of God, <u>on account of which the heavens will be
destroyed by burning, and the elements will melt with intense heat!
13 But according to His promise we are looking for new heavens
and a new earth, in which righteousness dwells.</u>*

THE RE-GRAFTING OF ISRAEL

Peter is reiterating the teachings of Jesus and of Paul, but since the
audience is Jewish, they are hearing it from Peter, whom they trust,
versus Paul who many distrusted. Paul's enemies had painted him as
an enemy of the Abrahamic Covenant. In fact, Peter specifically writes
to them that they should trust the teaching of *"our beloved brother,
Paul, who has already written to you"* (2 Pet 3:15). He is telling them
plainly that Paul's teaching on the Second Coming is scriptural, that
is, based in the Old Testament, which was the only Bible they had at
that time. The Second Coming is mainstream Jewish doctrine.

*2 Peter 3: 14 Therefore, beloved, since you look for these things,
be diligent to be found by Him in peace, spotless and blameless, 15
and regard the patience of our Lord to be salvation; <u>just as also our
beloved brother Paul, according to the wisdom given him, wrote to
you</u>, 16 as also in all his letters, speaking in them of these things,*

in which are some things hard to understand, which the untaught and unstable distort, as they do also the rest of the Scriptures, to their own destruction. 17 You therefore, beloved, knowing this beforehand, be on your guard lest, being carried away by the error of unprincipled men, you fall from your own steadfastness, 18 but grow in the grace and knowledge of our Lord and Savior Jesus Christ. To Him be the glory, both now and to the day of eternity. Amen (NAS)

Paul tells us in Romans that when Israel was cut off, God grafted the Gentiles, a wild olive branch, to the "root of His vine", his covenant promise to Abraham (Rom 11:15-24). This means God has made us sons of Abraham by adoption. He tells us that the Gentile church was a mystery, hidden in the ages, that was not seen by the Jews (Rom 11:25-27; Col 1:25-27; Eph 3:9-10). He goes on to say that we Gentiles benefited from their fall, but we should not get haughty, because God is going to re-graft Israel back into the stump of the vine (Rom 11:17-24).

Rom 11:15-24 For if their rejection be the reconciliation of the world, what will their acceptance be but life from the dead? 16 And if the first piece of dough be holy, the lump is also; and if the root be holy, the branches are too. 17 But if some of the branches were broken off, and you, being a wild olive, were grafted in among them and became partaker with them of the rich root of the olive tree, 18 do not be arrogant toward the branches; but if you are arrogant, remember that it is not you who supports the root, but the root supports you. 19 You will say then, "Branches were broken off so that I might be grafted in." 20 Quite right, they were broken off for their unbelief, but you stand by your faith. Do not be conceited, but fear; 21 for if God did not spare the natural branches, neither will He spare you. 22 Behold then the kindness and severity of God; to those who fell, severity, but to you, God's kindness, if you continue in His kindness; otherwise you also will be cut off. 23 And they also, if they do not continue in their unbelief, will be grafted in; for God is able to graft them in again. 24 For if you were cut off from what is by nature a wild olive tree, and were grafted contrary to nature into a cultivated olive tree, how much more shall these who are the natural branches be grafted into their own olive tree? (NAS)

The "age of the Gentiles" had a beginning and it will have an end. When God has determined that this age has been completed, He will turn His attention once again and restore His Jewish people. He will bring circumstances upon them that cause them to return to Him. He will allow them to find Him once more as a people. He will reestablish His covenant with them as a chosen people. (We covered this earlier in the section on the preeminence of Israel.) Those circumstances have become known as the Tribulation, the seven-year period that precedes the Second Coming.

That seven-year period is the last seven years of Daniel's prophetic 490 years (Dan 9:20-27). It is the end of time allotted for Daniel's people, Israel. That is why the "ripening of the fig tree" is seen as a bellwether event of the Second Coming. In fact, as we shall see later, it is after the Antichrist breaks his covenant with Israel and persecutes them unmercifully for 42 months that they cry out as a nation for the coming of their Messiah. It is that cry, the national plea from God's chosen people for salvation, that triggers the Second Coming of Christ, the Jewish Messiah.

Chapter 10

The Second Coming of the Messiah - Rapture and Resurrection

AT THE SECOND Coming of Jesus, the righteous will be given glorified bodies (1Cor 15:35-49); that is, they will be resurrected from the dead into new bodies. They will **not be merely reanimated** in their old pre-death physical bodies as were, for example, Lazarus (Jn 11), Jairus' daughter (Lk 9:49-56), the son of the widow of Nain (Lk 7:11-17) and Dorcas (Acts 9:36-42). There is a significant difference between resurrection and reanimation. Only Jesus has been resurrected from the dead so far. The rest of the righteous dead will be resurrected and receive their glorified bodies at the Second Coming. Lazarus and all others in the Bible who were "raised from the dead" were reanimated in their physical bodies and had to die again later. That is not true resurrection.

At the Second Coming, born-again believers will receive the type of bodies that Jesus received at His resurrection (1 Cor 15:35-44). His body could walk through closed doors (Jn 20:19-29), appear and vanish at will (Luke 24), but it could also eat fish (Lk 24:41-43; Jn 21:13) and it could be physically touched (Jn 20:26-29). It was at times corporeal and at other times non-corporeal. It was similar in appearance to the way Jesus looked before His resurrection, but somehow different enough in appearance to require some focus to recognize Him (Lk 24: 30-32; Jn 21:12).

The timing of the resurrection of the dead in Christ is clearly indicated in several places. It will occur at the Second Coming, an event which takes place at the end of the seven-year tribulation period.

> *1 Cor 15:22-26 For as in Adam all die, so also in Christ all shall be made alive, 23 but each in his own order: Christ the first fruits,* **_after that those who are Christ's at His coming._** *24 Then comes the end, when He delivers up the kingdom to the God and Father, when He has abolished all rule and all authority and power. 25 For He must reign until He has put all His enemies under His feet. 26 The last enemy that will be abolished is death. (NAS)*

Paul tells Timothy (see below) that he (Paul) and all other saints will receive crowns as part of their reward at the coming of Christ. In the Greco-Roman world of Paul's day, crowns were given to the victor in a wrestling match or a race. This is exactly like the gold medals we award the winners of athletic contests in our age. They were handed out at the "coming of the judge."

> *2 Tim 4:7-8 I have fought the good fight, I have finished the course, I have kept the faith. 8 In the future there is laid up for me the crown of righteousness, which the Lord, the righteous Judge, will award to me* **_on that day;_** *and not only to me, but also* **_to all who have loved His appearing_**. *(NAS)*

ANOTHER LOOK AT CREATION

Another indication of the timing of the resurrection of the dead is the restoration of the physical earth to its design, structure and function. Paul says that since man fell, the earth has been "*subjected to futility.*" It does not function the way it was intended to function. It is no longer configured as it was originally created. One view is that at Noah's flood, the bowels of the earth erupted (Gen 7:11), shifting the tectonic plates and creating seven distinct continents with huge mountains separated by huge troughs filled with water–the oceans. Modern scientists agree that this happened at some point–the severing of Pangaea from one large land mass into seven continents. Many of them doubt that it happened at Noah's flood, but they will agree that it happened sometime in the distant past.

In grade school Geography class, we were told that at one time all the continents were connected as one whole land mass known as Pangaea - Greek for whole earth or one big earth. The teacher would show you a large map of the world and point out that all the continents would fit rather nicely together if you could push them together (give or take a little bit for erosion). Based on the way modern science measures the age of physical objects such as the earth, the stars, etc., our teachers would tell us that this happened millions of years ago.

Creation scientists think that this happened at Noah's flood in about 2500B.C.. They subscribe to the "Young Earth Theory"–that the earth, as we know it, is only 7,000–10,000 years old. Evolutionists scoff, but every time science demonstrates additional complexity and implied design in the creation, evolutionists push their timeline back further and further. They have to do this to allow for the necessary time for that complexity to happen by accident, thus opening up huge and ever-increasing numbers of holes in their theory.

Some Creation scientists offer the following explanation in support of the Genesis account. God's creation of the earth on the First Day in Genesis was focused on creating order out of chaos and it resulted in the formation of an earth that was covered by water (Gen 1:1-5). The light and darkness referenced in these passages probably refer to illumination as opposed to physical light. The sun, moon and stars were not created until Day Four. In other words, on Day One God made sense out of chaos.

Then on Day Two, God separated the water from the land mass and created Pangaea below and a "canopy" of water above it (Gen 1:9-10). The Hebrew word is "rachiya" and is translated canopy, firmament or expanse. This canopy was then found above the earth in a connected liquid form providing the earth a terrarium-like environment with great similarity to a rain forest. Protected from the harmful rays and toxic energies of outer space, the planet grew and supported bounteous vegetation, large animals and long-lived men. The Bible tells us that before the flood, it did not rain on the earth, but a mist used to arise from the ground to water all things (Gen 2:6).

Adding in the creative events of Days Three-Six, we get the formation of the Garden of Eden.

Sin causes barriers (even enmity) to come between God and man and man and his neighbor. As sin progressed and man became more and more corrupt over the next 1700 years, their relationship with God became untenable and deteriorated continuously until God closed the door on Noah's ark and upon all mankind with the exception of Noah's family. Then an extraordinary geological event occurs as described briefly in Gen 7:11-12.

> *"All the fountains of the great deep burst open, and the floodgates of the sky were opened. 12 and the rain fell upon the earth for forty days and forty nights." (NAS)*

One of the theories of Creation Science is that there were great pockets of water trapped at the earth's core, put there by an all-knowing God and awaiting the appointed foreknown hour. Over time this trapped water became heated to ever-increasing temperatures until at that appointed hour they reached a critical temperature creating enough force to shift the tectonic plates, ripping Pangaea apart and forcing great mountains upward into the sky. Having been trapped under increasing and enormous counter pressure (the earth's mass), that water shot upward in white hot geysers that reached and subsequently melted the "rachiyah," a Hebrew word meaning the "canopy" of water put there by God on Day Two of creation. This caused the "rachiyah" to fall to the earth with such mass and force as to strip the earth bare to its rocky bones and flush all living things toward the poles and to a watery grave. Over time these waters, having cleansed the earth of mankind and his culture of sin, and violence, settled down into the great canyons created by the shifting of the tectonic plates forming the oceans as we know them today.

Then God blew His breath upon the waters causing a wind to pass over the waters and they receded (Gen 8:1). The Creation scientists would tell you that this process would cause some of the water to evaporate, rise up into the atmosphere as a lighter gas. Then it would re-condense in the cooler temperatures of that atmosphere until it became heavy enough for gravity to pull it back to the earth's surface.

This would form the rain cycle that we know today - the earth's "new normal."

Evolutionists argue from the point of measured time. The earth, the heavens, the layered fossil record demonstrate that these cataclysmic event did happen, but must have happened over millions of years and cannot have happened as they are portrayed in the Genesis timeline. Let's assume that the age-measuring devices are accurate. That still does not deny the Genesis account and here is an explanation that addresses the argument.

Suppose you were a doctor and you gave Adam and Eve physical exams, shortly after they were each created by God. Your report would say something like, "Adult male and female with normal development in all organs: e.g., normal maturational signs, puberty reached, all baby teeth gone, etc." Your evaluation as a professional physician would be spot on, but that would not prevent them from just having been created last week as adults. This is called "implied time." If Genesis is accurate, God would have created in "implied time." He made the earth fully formed and developed. He created Adam and Eve as adults. The scientific measurements may be accurate, but they do NOT disprove Genesis.

When He created fish and birds, they would have been of all ages. In fact, He could have created multiple generations at one time. Genesis 1:20-23 says that on Day Five *"God created the great sea monsters, and every living creature that moves, <u>with which the waters swarmed</u> after their kind, and every winged bird after its kind; and God saw that it was good."* This means that God created in volume as well as with implied time.

We are also told that God *"stretches out the heavens"* (Job 9:8) and spread out the stars indicating that God "created in motion" as well as in volume and with implied time. So measure all of that with whatever instruments you like. If you say, "My measuring devices tell me the light of that star has been traveling to earth for millions of years," God could reply, "I know. I created it already on its way." Even though we may not fully understand the answers, it does not follow, therefore, that the answers do not exist. Science does not have to conflict with the Bible.

Whether or not you believe the Genesis story, it was the foundational belief of Jesus, the apostles, the writers of the Gospel, Paul and indeed all writers of both the Old and New Testaments, including the prophets–maybe especially the prophets. And that is why it is germane to our discussion of the Eschaton, because many of these writers tell us that *all of the original creation will be restored at the Second Coming.* We will again see Pangaea, the Garden and the undoing of the damages of Noah's Flood. In the same way that Adam's sin destroyed the relationship between man and God and between man and the earth, Jesus' return will reconcile them all. The barriers will come down on all levels, including the geological barriers. There will be more on this in the section on the Millennial Reign and there are numerous scriptures in support of this in Appendix III: The Themes of Isaiah under "Mountains and Valleys Rearranged" and a "Highway in the Desert."

Now let's get back to our discussion of the Second Coming of Christ. As I was saying earlier, another indication of the timing of the resurrection of the dead is the restoration of the physical earth to its designed structure and function. Paul says that since man fell the earth has been *"subjected to futility."* It does not work right. It does not function the way it was supposed to function. It is not even configured as it was created. Paul's comments in Romans 8:19-23 anthropomorphize the earth and allow it to "express" its sense of frustration with the poor stewardship of mankind that has subjected it (the earth) to futility. The earth "groans" until it is fully restored and allowed to function as it was intended. This restorative event occurs along with the redemption of the bodies of the righteous at the Second Coming of Christ.

> *Rom 8:19-23 For the anxious longing of the creation waits eagerly for the revealing of the sons of God. 20 For the creation was subjected to futility, not of its own will, but because of Him who subjected it, in hope 21 that the creation itself also will be set free from its slavery to corruption into the freedom of the glory of the children of God. 22 For we know that the whole creation groans and suffers the pains of childbirth together until now. 23 And not only this, but also we ourselves, having the first fruits of the Spirit,*

even we ourselves groan within ourselves, waiting eagerly for our
adoption as sons, the redemption of our body. (NAS)

In the same way that the earth was broken in a cataclysmic
geological struggle at the time of Noah's flood, it will be restored in
a cataclysmic geological struggle associated with the return of the
Lord. If that happens as prophesied, it will certainly be a sign of His
coming. More on this in the following chapter entitled The Day of
the Lord.

THE RAPTURE OF THE BELIEVERS

1 Cor 15:51-53 Behold, I tell you a mystery; we shall not all sleep,
*but **we shall all be changed, 52 in a moment, in the twinkling of***
an eye, at the last trumpet; for the trumpet will sound, and the
***dead will be raised imperishable, and we shall be changed**. 53*
For this perishable must put on the imperishable, and this mortal
must put on immortality. (NAS)

The saints of God who have already gone to be with God (died) by
the time of the Second Coming will return with Jesus when He comes
again. The born-again believers who are alive on the earth at the time
of His coming will be "**caught up** to meet Him in the air," an event
known as the Rapture (from the Latin "raptura" translated as "caught
up"). This word is also used to describe several other Biblical events;
e.g., the catching up of Philip in Acts 8:39, the catching up of Paul
in 1 Cor 12:2-4, and the catching up of the Male Child in Revelation
12:5. First Corinthians 15:23 places the Rapture of the saints at the
time of the seventh trumpet in Revelation 11:15.

1 Thess 4:14-18 For if we believe that Jesus died and rose again,
even so God will bring with Him those who have fallen asleep in
Jesus. 15 For this we say to you by the word of the Lord, that we
who are alive, and remain until the coming of the Lord, shall not
precede those who have fallen asleep. 16 For the Lord Himself will
descend from heaven with a shout, with the voice of the archangel,
*and **with the trumpet of God**; and the dead in Christ shall rise first.*
*17 Then we who are alive and remain shall be **caught up together***

__with them in the clouds to meet the Lord in the air__, and thus we shall always be with the Lord. 18 Therefore comfort one another with these words. (NAS)

Jesus Himself spoke of this event as a literal event in time and space.

Mt 24:29 "But immediately after the tribulation of those days the sun will be darkened, and the moon will not give its light, and the stars will fall from the sky, and the powers of the heavens will be shaken, 30 and then the sign of the Son of Man will appear in the sky, and then all the tribes of the earth will mourn, and they will see the Son of Man coming on the clouds of the sky with power and great glory. 31 __"And He will send forth His angels with a great trumpet and they will gather together His elect from the four winds, from one end of the sky to the other__. (NAS)

All of these scriptures have one thing in common. They assume that the <u>Rapture of the Church</u> will happen at the Second Coming of Jesus. The Rapture will be yet another sign of His coming. Contrary to popular fiction, this "Rapture" will occur at the Second Coming of Jesus, not in any "Pre-Tribulation" or "Mid-Tribulation" period.

The "Rapture" is a Biblical doctrine that is the source of no little controversy in the modern church. That the Bible speaks of a Rapture is indisputable for evangelicals (Bible believers). While it is true that liberal scholars may challenge the literal nature of the Rapture, they also have been known to challenge the literal nature of the Creation story, the Millennial Reign of Christ upon the earth, the Virgin Birth, the Resurrection of Jesus and the divinity of Christ. Our work neither seeks to convince liberals nor to exhaustively address their thinking. We seek only to provide evangelical laymen Biblical support for concepts related to the Eschaton (end times).

The controversy among evangelicals is not that there is a Rapture, but when it will occur. The Rapture is a feature or a subset of the Resurrection of the Dead. Traditionally and historically, when the church has addressed the Rapture at all, it was seen as an event occurring at the time of the Second Coming of Christ. According to

1 Cor 15: 21-24, Paul taught that resurrection of the righteous dead (and the Rapture) occurred "at His coming." He is even clearer in 1 Thess 4:14-18 telling us that all the righteous dead will return with Jesus for the purpose of resurrection and that those living at that time will be "caught up to meet Him in the air." The Latin term for "caught up" is *raptura* from which we get the term Rapture. Paul tells Timothy that he is ready to die and go to be with the Lord and that he expects to receive his crown "at His appearing" (2 Tim 4:8). For 1800 years of church history, that is how the church read the scriptures on this subject.

In about 1830 a doctrine arose in Britain suggesting that the Rapture would occur at the beginning of the Tribulation. It was promulgated by Margaret MacDonald, John Darby and the Plymouth Brethren to support the idea that God would not allow his beloved children to suffer the seven-year Tribulation period. This became known as Pre-Tribulation Rapture theory. It found no broad support and would probably have gone nowhere except that it was picked up by Cyrus Ingerson Scofield, the author of an extraordinarily popular reference work on the King James Version of the Bible in 1909 and revised in 1917. It then received the support of Pre-Trib rapturists in Bible conferences, Bible colleges and Fundamentalist seminaries. It began to be espoused by John Walvoord, John Ryrie and Dwight Pentecost, men of influence and character.

In the 1940s, men began to preach a compromise known as Mid-Trib Rapture theory. It suggested (correctly) that God would not subject his church and his people to His Wrath. They taught the wrath would fall upon the earth during the entire last 3.5 years of the Tribulation and, therefore, necessitated a Mid-Trib Rapture of the saints. Our study of the scripture persuades us that the Wrath of God falls upon the earth at the Second Coming at the end of the seven-year Tribulation period pushing the Rapture back to that same time.

For 1800 years the fathers of the church believed in a Post-Tribulation Pre-Wrath Rapture. These included even the more modern reformers and church fathers such as Wesley, Calvin, Spurgeon, Knox, Hus, William Carey, George Whitfield, Wycliffe, Bunyan, A.B. Simspon and many others. The concept of a Pre-Trib or Mid-Trib

Rapture is relatively new and does not stand up under scriptural scrutiny by open-minded investigators. For a more in-depth discussion of this subject, I recommend The Pre-Wrath Rapture of the Church by Marvin Rosenthal (ISBN 0-8407-7499-0). He is a leading Messianic Jew and a graduate of Dallas Theological Seminary. Unlike this work, his is a scholarly treatise that covers the thinking of numerous other scholars in the field over time. In addition to making a solid case, he offers an in-depth bibliography. I am indebted to his work to help me in my own studies.

The Tribulation period is the seven years immediately prior to the Second Coming of Jesus. Jesus tells us that they will be VERY difficult days (see Mark 13 below).

> *Mark 13:19-20* **"*For those days will be a time of tribulation such as has not occurred since the beginning of the creation which God created, until now, and never shall*** *. 20 "And unless the Lord had shortened those days, no life would have been saved; but for the sake of the elect whom He chose, He shortened the days. (NAS)*

During this time the world will come under the sway (even control) of a dynamic but deceptive leader the Bible calls the Antichrist, the man of lawlessness and the man of iniquity. Daniel prophesied that this period would last seven years and that the first three and one-half years would be a time of a false worldwide peace and a false covenant between the Antichrist and the people of Israel. **In the middle of the seven-year Tribulation period**, the Antichrist will break his covenant with Israel and launch an attack of genocidal proportions and intent. It is this sustained three and one-half year attack upon the people of Israel that will cause them to cry out to God in desperation for the coming of the promised Messiah. God's answer will be the Second Coming of Christ. These events are also signs that precede the Second Coming.

> *Mark 13:24-27* *"But in those days, **after that tribulation**, the sun will be darkened, and the moon will not give its light, 25 and the stars will be falling from heaven, and the powers that are in the*

*heavens will be shaken. 26 "**And then they will see the Son of Man***
***coming in clouds with great power and glory**. 27 "And then He*
will send forth the angels, and will gather together His elect from
the four winds, from the farthest end of the earth, to the farthest
end of heaven. (NAS)

There has been much speculation and supposition concerning
many events and scenarios associated with this period. Some have
speculated that God will perform a miraculous rescue of all born-
again people on the earth to prevent them from having to endure
this Tribulation in whole or in part. Some have suggested that this
"Rapture of the believers" will occur at the beginning of the seven-
year Tribulation period. This theory is known as the **Pre-Tribulation
Rapture** theory. Others surmise that this "Rapture of the believers"
will occur in the middle of the seven-year Tribulation period. This
theory is known as the **Mid-Tribulation Rapture** theory. Although
these speculative theories are popular, they are not Biblically supported as will be demonstrated herein. The "Rapture" of the believers,
as this event is known, actually occurs at the Second Coming of Christ
at the end of the Great Tribulation.

1 Cor 15:20-26 But now Christ has been raised from the dead, the
first fruits of those who are asleep. 21 For since by a man came
death, by a man also came the resurrection of the dead. 22 For as in
*Adam all die, so also in Christ all shall be made alive. 23 **But each***
in his own order: Christ the first fruits, after that those who are
***Christ's at His coming,** 24 then comes the end, when He delivers*
up the kingdom to the God and Father, when He has abolished all
rule and all authority and power. 25 For He must reign until He
has put all His enemies under His feet. 26 The last enemy that will
be abolished is death. (NAS)

2 Tim 4:7-8 I have fought the good fight, I have finished the course,
I have kept the faith; 8 in the future there is laid up for me the
crown of righteousness, which the Lord, the righteous Judge, will
award to me on that day; and not only to me, but also to all who
have loved His appearing. (NAS)

*1 Thess 4:13-18 But we do not want you to be uninformed, brethren, about those who are asleep, that you may not grieve, as do the rest who have no hope. 14 For if we believe that Jesus died and rose again, even so God will bring with Him those who have fallen asleep in Jesus. 15 For this we say to you by the word of the Lord, that we who are alive, and remain until the coming of the Lord, shall not precede those who have fallen asleep. 16 For the Lord Himself will descend from heaven with a shout, with the voice of the archangel, and with the trumpet of God; and the dead in Christ shall rise first. 17 Then we who are alive and remain shall **be caught up together with them in the clouds to meet the Lord in the air**, and thus we shall always be with the Lord. 18 Therefore comfort one another with these words. (NAS)*

Jesus' comment in the three gospels concerning "two men in a field and one is taken" is erroneously used to support a Pre-Tribulation or Mid-Tribulation Rapture. However, in spite of popular fiction, this event occurs after the seven-year Tribulation but before the Wrath of God at the Second Coming of Christ.

*Matt 24:36-42 "For **the coming of the Son of Man** will be just like the days of Noah. 38 "For as in those days which were before the flood they were eating and drinking, they were marrying and giving in marriage, until the day that Noah entered the ark, 39 and they did not understand until the flood came and took them all away; so shall the coming of the Son of Man be. 40 "Then there shall be <u>two men in the field; one will be taken</u>, and one will be left. 41 "<u>Two women will be grinding at the mill; one will be taken,</u> and one will be left. (NAS)*

Matt 13:24-30 He (Jesus) presented another parable to them, saying, "The kingdom of heaven may be compared to a man who sowed good seed in his field. 25 "But while men were sleeping, his enemy came and sowed tares also among the wheat, and went away. 26 "But when the wheat sprang up and bore grain, then the tares became evident also. 27 "And the slaves of the landowner came and said to him, 'Sir, did you not sow good seed in your field? How then does it have tares?' 28 "And he said to them, 'An enemy *has done this!' And the slaves said to him, 'Do you want us, then, to go and gather them up?' 29 "But he said, 'No; lest while you are gathering up the tares, you may root up the wheat with them. 30'**Allow both to grow together until the harvest**; and in the time of the harvest I will say to the reapers, "First gather up the tares and bind them in bundles to burn them up; but gather the wheat into my barn."' (NAS)*

At the time of the end, the church (body of Christ) will be purged of all unbelievers and lukewarm attendees. The tares (weeds) will be taken out so the church will be purified, strengthened and prepared to endure the Tribulation. In fact, it is usually persecution that causes the unbelievers and the lukewarm to "abandon the pretense" of Christian commitment. Jesus tells them that only at the time of the harvest can one truly determine what is "wheat" and what is "weed." Up until that time, they often look the same. So when He speaks of "waiting until the Harvest to separate the wheat from the tares," he is talking about the purging of the eschatological church, not the Rapture. The lukewarm churchgoers will be vomited out of His mouth as He tells the Laodicean church. (Rev 3:14-16)

HE WHO ENDURES WILL BE SAVED

Finally, we need to see that both Jesus and John the Revelator have a single theme embedded in their messages. **They both tell us to be prepared to endure**. They do not tell us to be prepared to be rescued. The purpose of all eschatological prophecy is **to encourage us to endure.** This precludes the purpose or need for a Pre-Trib or Mid-Trib Rapture.

Matt 24:9-13 "Then they will deliver you to tribulation, and will kill you, and you will be hated by all nations on account of My name. 10 "And at that time many will fall away and will deliver up one another and hate one another. 11 "And many false prophets will arise, and will mislead many. 12 "And because lawlessness is increased, most people's love will grow cold. 13 "But the one who endures to the end, he shall be saved. (NAS)

*Matt 24:42-51 "Therefore be on the alert, for you do not know which day your Lord is coming. 43 "But be sure of this, that if the head of the house had known at what time of the night the thief was coming, he would have been on the alert and would not have allowed his house to be broken into. 44 "For this reason you be ready too; for the Son of Man is coming at an hour when you do not think He will. 45 "Who then is the faithful and sensible slave whom his master put in charge of his household to give them their food at the proper time? 46 "**Blessed is that slave whom his master finds so doing when he comes**. 47 "Truly I say to you, that he will put him in charge of all his possessions. 48 "But if that evil slave says in his heart, 'My master is not coming for a long time,' 49 and shall begin to beat his fellow slaves and eat and drink with drunkards; 50 the master of that slave will come on a day when he does not expect him and at an hour which he does not know, 51 and shall cut him in pieces and assign him a place with the hypocrites; weeping shall be there and the gnashing of teeth. (NAS)*

*1 Cor 4:11-13 To this present hour we are both hungry and thirsty, and are poorly clothed, and are roughly treated, and are homeless; 12 and we toil, working with our own hands; when we are reviled, we bless; **when we are persecuted, we endure**; 13 when we are slandered, we try to conciliate; we have become as the scum of the world, the dregs of all things, even until now. (NAS)*

2 Thess 1:3-4 We ought always to give thanks to God for you, brethren, as is only fitting, because your faith is greatly enlarged, and the love of each one of you toward one another grows ever greater; 4 therefore, we ourselves speak proudly of you among the churches of God for your perseverance and faith in the midst of all your persecutions and afflictions which you endure. (NAS)

2 Tim 2:8-13 Remember Jesus Christ, risen from the dead, descendant of David, according to my gospel, 9 for which I suffer hardship even to imprisonment as a criminal; but the word of God is not imprisoned. 10 For this reason I endure all things for the sake of those who are chosen, that they also may obtain the salvation which is in Christ Jesus and with it eternal glory. 11 It is a trustworthy statement: for if we died with Him, we shall also *live with Him. 12 **If we endure, we shall also reign with Him.** If we deny Him, He also will deny us. 13 If we are faithless, He remains faithful; for He cannot deny Himself.* (NAS)

*Heb 11:23-26 By faith Moses, when he was born, was hidden for three months by his parents, because they saw he was a beautiful child; and they were not afraid of the king's edict. 24 By faith Moses, when he had grown up, refused to be called the son of Pharaoh's daughter; **25 choosing rather to endure ill-treatment with the people of God**, than to enjoy the passing pleasures of sin; 26 considering the reproach of Christ greater riches than the treasures of Egypt; for he was looking to the reward.* (NAS)

*James 1:2-4 Consider it all joy, my brethren, when you encounter various trials, 3 knowing that **the testing of your faith produces endurance.** 4 And **let endurance have its perfect result**, that you may be perfect and complete, lacking in nothing.* (NAS)

*1 Peter 2:20 For what credit is there if, when you sin and are harshly treated, you endure it with patience? **But if when you do what is right and suffer for it you patiently endure it, this finds favor with God.*** (NAS)

Chapter 11

The Day of the Lord

ONE OF THE most significant events of the Eschaton is "The Day of the Lord." It is a point of focus by both Old Testament prophets, New Testament writers and of Jesus Himself. It begins at the Second Coming of Christ and the Rapture of God's people. It is a time of the most significant worldwide judgment since Noah's flood and is compared to it in scope and intensity. It is a period of time in which the people of the world will be judged for their sins and in which the people of Israel will be purged from sin. It is a period of the Wrath of God upon the earth. When the Day of the Lord is finished, there will be a new heaven and a new earth and the Millennial Reign will begin.

> *2 Peter 3:8-9 But do not let this one fact escape your notice, beloved, that with the Lord one day is as a thousand years, and a thousand years as one day. 9 The Lord is not slow about His promise, as some count slowness, but is patient toward you, not wishing for any to perish but for all to come to repentance. (NAS)*

As we have discussed previously, God has been (and often is) faulted for allowing the sin of man to go on and on and to progress in both evil and scope. Why, they ask, does God not come back and clean up this mess and punish the evil ones in the world? Peter tells us that God is not asleep or inattentive but that He is VERY patient so that more people can be saved and share His Heaven. To God, a thousand years is jut like one day to us. In the scope of eternity,

Jesus' delay in returning is not really a long time. Our children cry out in anxious longing for Christmas to come or summer vacation to begin. To them the wait seems interminable. Yet we know that it is really not a long time, that there is much to accomplish until then and that our children lack patience. So it is with God and the Second Coming. He is patient because He wants all of the foreknown saved ones to have time to repent. However, when He finally **IS** done with waiting, Jesus will return with awesome terrifying judgment upon the earth and its people. The Wrath of God will be poured out as never before in fiery destruction in a short period known in the Bible as "The Day of The Lord." When it comes, it will catch everyone by surprise except the true Christians.

> *2 Peter 3:10-13 But the day of the Lord will come like a thief, in which the **heavens will pass away with a roar and the elements will be destroyed with intense heat, and the earth and its works will be burned up**. 11 Since all these things are to be destroyed in this way, what sort of people ought you to be in holy conduct and godliness, 12 looking for and hastening the coming of the day of God, on account of which **the heavens will be destroyed by burning, and the elements will melt with intense heat**! 13 But according to His promise we are looking for new heavens and a new earth, in which righteousness dwells. (NAS)*

There is a great cosmic disturbance associated with the beginning of the Day of the Lord. The Bible speaks of it here and in numerous other passages. It will have the scope of Noah's flood, but it will be associated with fire, not water. As with Noah's flood, it will eliminate most but not all of the world's population. Its function will be to cleanse the human race, not destroy it. It will allow the world to start over again under the "second Adam" when, in its aftermath, Jesus begins His Millennial Reign upon the earth. And it will come when the world is not expecting it, suddenly, surprisingly like "a thief in the night." Jesus Himself explains it thus:

> *Matt 24:37-39 "For the coming of the Son of Man will be just like the days of Noah. 38 "For as in those days which were before the flood they were eating and drinking, they were marrying and giving*

in marriage, until the day that Noah entered the ark, 39 and they did not understand until the flood came and took them all away; so shall the coming of the Son of Man be. (NAS)

In 2 Peter 3 which we began to discuss above, Peter goes on to tell us we should anticipate the Coming of the Lord because the scriptures have clearly foretold it and that we should live righteously in anticipation of its imminence. We should think of God's patience as a mechanism of salvation and not think of it as God's slipshod or careless management of His creation. We should avoid the faulty, arrogant teachings of men that both impugn God's stewardship and distort the truth about these events. Jesus is coming again soon. He will Rapture His church when He does come and His coming will usher in the Day of the Lord, the most horrible judgment ever seen, the Wrath of God upon unbelieving and unrepentant mankind. (See the following.)

2 Peter 3:14-18 Therefore, beloved, since you look for these things, be diligent to be found by Him in peace, spotless and blameless, 15 and regard the patience of our Lord to be salvation; just as also our beloved brother Paul, according to the wisdom given him, wrote to you, 16 as also in all his letters, speaking in them of these things, in which are some things hard to understand, which the untaught and unstable distort, as they do also the rest of the Scriptures, to their own destruction. 17 You therefore, beloved, knowing this beforehand, be on your guard lest, being carried away by the error of unprincipled men, you fall from your own steadfastness, 18 but grow in the grace and knowledge of our Lord and Savior Jesus Christ. To Him be the glory, both now and to the day of eternity. Amen. (NAS)

In this next section, we will talk about the Day of the Lord, the Wrath of God, the Rapture of the Church and the Second Coming of Christ all of which are coterminous in time. We do Christians a great disservice by suggesting anything other than this as it relates to the Rapture. For although the church is not "appointed to Wrath," it will have to endure the Great Tribulation and it needs to prepare itself by holy living.

What does the scripture say about the Day of the Lord? The prophets foretold it. The New Testament writers confirmed their belief in it and Jesus addressed it as a most important future event that we must anticipate and for which we must prepare.

ISAIAH

Isaiah calls it a day of worldwide terror, cosmic upheaval and judgment.

> *Isa 13:6-12 Wail, for the **Day of the LORD is near**! It will come as destruction from the Almighty. 7 Therefore all hands will fall limp, and every man's heart will melt. 8 And they will be terrified. Pains and anguish will take hold of them. They will writhe like a woman in labor. They will look at one another in astonishment, their faces aflame. 9 Behold, the **Day of the LORD is coming**, cruel, with fury and burning anger, to make the land a desolation; and He will exterminate its sinners from it. 10 For the stars of heaven and their constellations will not flash forth their light. The sun will be dark when it rises, and the moon will not shed its light. 11 Thus I will punish the world for its evil, and the wicked for their iniquity. I will also put an end to the arrogance of the proud, and abase the haughtiness of the ruthless. 12 **I will make mortal man scarcer than pure gold**, and mankind than the gold of Ophir. (NAS)*

In the Day of the Lord every man's heart will melt (worldwide terror), and men will writhe like a woman in labor. Jesus and Paul both use this analogy from Isaiah in talking about the events leading up to the Second Coming (Mt 24:8, 1Thess 5:3). He will exterminate sinners and punish the world for its evil. He will put an end to arrogance and make men scarcer than gold. There will be a great cosmic disturbance in that day.

EZEKIEL

Ezekiel calls it a day of battle, of doom for the nations (Ez 13:3-5; 30:3).

Ezek 13:3-5 'Thus says the Lord GOD, "Woe to the foolish prophets who are following their own spirit and have seen nothing. 4 "O Israel, your prophets have been like foxes among ruins. 5 "You have not gone up into the breaches, nor did you build the wall around the house of Israel to stand in the battle on the day of the LORD. (NAS)

Ezek 30:3-4 "For the day is near, even the day of the LORD is near. It will be a day of clouds, a time of doom for the nations. 4 "And a sword will come upon Egypt, and anguish will be in Ethiopia, when the slain fall in Egypt, they take away her wealth, and her foundations are torn down. (NAS)

JOEL

Joel calls it a day of "destruction from the Almighty" (Joel 1:15). The nations will tremble before the great army of God <u>at the sound of the trumpet</u>. Joel coins images later used by Jesus, Paul and John, images of fire consuming the earth, a thief in the night and a cosmic disturbance in the heavens. These are the images of the six trumpet judgments of the Day of the Lord in Revelation chapters eight and nine and the seventh trumpet in Rev 11:15.

*Joel 2:1-11 Blow a trumpet in Zion, and sound an alarm on My holy mountain! Let all the inhabitants of the land tremble, for the day of the LORD is coming. Surely it is near, 2 a day of darkness and gloom, a day of clouds and thick darkness. As the dawn is spread over the mountains, so there is a great and mighty people. There has never been anything like it, nor will there be again after it to the years of many generations. 3 **A fire consumes before them, and behind them a flame burns**. The land is like the Garden of Eden before them, but a desolate wilderness behind them, and nothing at all escapes them. 4 Their appearance is like the appearance of horses; and like war horses, so they run. 5 With a noise as of chariots they leap on the tops of the mountains. Like the crackling of a flame of fire consuming the stubble, like a mighty people arranged for battle. 6 Before them the people are in anguish. All faces turn pale. 7 They run like mighty men. They climb the wall like soldiers; and they each march in line, nor do they deviate from their paths.*

8 They do not crowd each other. They march everyone in his path. When they burst through the defenses, they do not break ranks. 9 They rush on the city, they run on the wall. They climb into the houses. **They enter through the windows like a thief. 10 Before them the earth quakes. The heavens tremble. The sun and the moon grow dark, and the stars lose their brightness.** *11 And the LORD utters His voice before His army. Surely His camp is very great, for strong is he who carries out His word. The day of the LORD is indeed great and very awesome, and who can endure it?* (NAS)

In the Day of the Lord, Jesus will shelter His born-again followers (the Rapture of the church) and fight for His people Israel.

Joel 3:12-16 Let the nations be aroused and come up to the valley of Jehoshaphat. For there I will sit to judge all the surrounding nations. 13 Put in the sickle, for the harvest is ripe. Come, tread, for the wine press is full. The vats overflow, for their wickedness is great. 14 Multitudes, multitudes in the valley of decision! For the **Day of the LORD** *is near in the valley of decision.* **15 The sun and moon grow dark, and the stars lose their brightness. 16 And the LORD roars from Zion and utters His voice from Jerusalem, and the heavens and the earth tremble**. *But the LORD is a refuge for His people and a stronghold to the sons of Israel.* (NAS)

AMOS AND MALACHI

Amos (like Malachi after him) tells Israel they should not cry out for the day of the Lord so eagerly, because it will be a day of purging. It will not be fun.

Amos 5:18-20 Alas, you who are longing for the day of the LORD, for what purpose will the day of the LORD be to you? It will be darkness and not light; 19 As when a man flees from a lion, and a bear meets him, or goes home, leans his hand against the wall, and a snake bites him. 20 Will not the day of the LORD be darkness instead of light, even gloom with no brightness in it? (NAS)

*Mal 3:1-6 "Behold, I am going to send My messenger, and he will clear the way before Me. And the Lord, whom you seek, will suddenly come to His temple; and the messenger of the covenant, in whom you delight, behold, He is coming," says the LORD of hosts. 2 "***But who can endure the day of His coming***? And who can stand when He appears? For ***He is like a refiner's fire and like fullers' soap***. 3 "And He will sit as a smelter and purifier of silver, and He will purify the sons of Levi and refine them like gold and silver, so that they may present to the LORD offerings in righteousness. 4 "Then the offering of Judah and Jerusalem will be pleasing to the LORD, as in the days of old and as in former years. 5 "Then ***(in the Day of the Lord)*** I will draw near to you for judgment; and I will be a swift witness against the sorcerers and against the adulterers and against those who swear falsely, and against those who oppress the wage earner in his wages, the widow and the orphan, and those who turn aside the alien, and do not fear Me," says the LORD of hosts. 6 "For I, the LORD, do not change; therefore you, O sons of Jacob, are not consumed. (NAS)*

All men must be cleansed of sin in order to enter into the presence of God. If we accept Jesus as our substitutionary sacrifice and take upon us His righteousness, we will be made clean. But if not, we will face Him in the Day of the Lord. The Raptured church will have accepted Him and thus they will be **saved FROM** the Day of the Lord. Israel will not accept Him until they cry out for His deliverance so they must be **saved IN** the Day of the Lord. The followers of the Antichrist will be **judged BY** the Day of the Lord.

Obadiah tells us that the nations will reap what they have sown in the Day of the Lord.

Obad 15 "For the day of the LORD draws near on all the nations. As you have done, it will be done to you. Your dealings will return on your own head. (NAS)

ZEPHANIAH

Zephaniah tells us that the Day of the Lord will be a time of wrath upon the nations.

Zeph 1:14-18 Near is the great day of the LORD, near and coming very quickly. Listen, the day of the LORD! In it the warrior cries out bitterly. 15 **A day of wrath is that day***, a day of trouble and distress, a day of destruction and desolation, a day of darkness and gloom, a day of clouds and thick darkness, 16 a day of trumpet and battle cry, against the fortified cities and the high corner towers. 17 And I will bring distress on men, so that they will walk like the blind, because they have sinned against the LORD; and their blood will be poured out like dust, and their flesh like dung. 18 Neither their silver nor their gold will be able to deliver them on the day of the Lord's wrath. And* **all the earth will be devoured in the fire of His jealousy***, for* **He will make a complete end, indeed a terrifying one, of all the inhabitants of the earth***. (NAS)*

MALACHI

Malachi tells us the Day of the Lord will be "great and terrible" and will mark the return of Elijah. Zachary was told by the angel in the temple that his son John would come in the spirit of Elijah and prepare the way for the Messiah (Luke 1:17) in fulfillment of Malachi's prophecy. Jesus said that John the Baptist came in the Spirit of Elijah to prepare the way for his First Coming (Mk 9:11-13). Elijah is expected to come again before the Second Coming as well. On the Mount of Transfiguration, the disciples saw Jesus and Moses and Elijah talking to one another about the Second Coming.

Mal 4:5-6 "Behold, I am going to send you Elijah the prophet before the coming of the great and terrible day of the LORD. 6 "And he will restore the hearts of the fathers to their children, and the hearts of the children to their fathers, lest I come and smite the land with a curse." (NAS)

Paul, agreeing with the prophets, tells us that the Day of the Lord will come "like a thief in the night," that it will be a time of great distress, even "birth pangs," and that the world will not escape its wrath.

1 Thess 5:1-3 Now as to the times and the epochs, brethren, you have no need of anything to be written to you. 2 For you yourselves know full well that the day of the Lord will come just like a thief in the night. 3 While they are saying, "Peace and safety!" then destruction will come upon them suddenly like birth pangs upon a woman with child; and they shall not escape. (NAS)

Peter also quotes the prophets concerning the details of the Day of the Lord, the suddenness of its coming and the cosmic disturbances.

*2 Peter 3:10-13 But **the day of the Lord will come like a thief**, in which the heavens will pass away with a roar and the elements will be destroyed with intense heat, and the earth and its works will be burned up. 11 Since all these things are to be destroyed in this way, what sort of people ought you to be in holy conduct and godliness, 12 looking for and hastening the coming of the day of God, on account of which the heavens will be destroyed by burning, and the elements will melt with intense heat! 13 But according to His promise we are looking for new heavens and a new earth, in which righteousness dwells. (NAS)*

Jesus Himself bears witness to the prophets and their words. The Day of the Lord will come "like a thief in the night."

*Matt 24:42-44 "Therefore be on the alert, for you do not know which day your Lord is coming. 43 "But be sure of this, that if the head of the house had known at what time of the night the thief was coming, he would have been on the alert and would not have allowed his house to be broken into. 44 "For this reason you be ready too; **for the Son of Man is coming at an hour when you do not think He will**. (NAS)*

Jesus tells the people in Sardis in Revelation 3:3 that He is coming suddenly like a thief to judge sin in the earth, including in the church. In Rev 16:15 he speaks of "the day of God" as a day of war in which He will come like a thief.

THE WRATH OF GOD COMES AFTER THE TRIBULATION

The Day of the Lord will follow immediately upon the Second Coming of Christ and the Rapture of the church that occurs "*at His coming.*" It will be a day of great Wrath, of God's judgment upon the earth.

The wrath of God is His righteous anger that breaks out against all sin to defend and protect God's holiness. It is not so much directed at people as it is directed at unholiness and sin. It will, however destroy those people who cling to their unholiness and sin. In the Eschaton, the Wrath is a period of time and activity wherein God brings judgment down upon the Antichrist, his followers and all who have rejected Christ. While there is no Biblical reason to believe that Christians will be spared the Tribulation, the scripture does tell us that the church "is not appointed for wrath."

1 Thess 1:10 ...and to wait for His Son from heaven, whom He raised from the dead, that is Jesus, who <u>delivers us from the wrath to come</u>. (NAS)

1 Thess 5:9 For God hath not appointed us to wrath, but to obtain salvation by our Lord Jesus Christ. (KJV)

Jesus tells us that while we are in the world, we will have tribulation (Jn 16:33). He tells us we must endure the tribulation.

*Matt 24:9-14 "Then <u>they will deliver you to tribulation, and will kill you</u>, and you will be hated by all nations on account of My name. 10 "And at that time many will fall away and <u>will deliver up one another</u> and hate one another. 11 "And many false prophets will arise, and will mislead many. 12 "And because lawlessness is increased, most people's love will grow cold. 13 "But **<u>the one who endures to the end, he shall be saved</u>**. (NAS)*

He tells us it is the worst tribulation the world has ever seen or will ever see again. Mercifully, Jesus will cut those days short for the sake of the elect, hence the Rapture at the Second Coming.

*Matt 24:21-22 for then there will be <u>a great tribulation</u>, such as has not occurred since the beginning of the world until now, nor ever shall. 22 "And unless those days had been cut short, no life would have been saved; but **for the sake of the elect those days shall be cut short**. (NAS)*

At that point the cosmic disturbance associated with the Day of the Lord will occur, the trumpet will sound, Jesus will appear and the Rapture will happen.

*Matt 24:29-31 "But immediately after the tribulation of those days <u>the sun will be darkened, and the moon will not give its light, and the stars will fall from the sky, and the powers of the heavens will be shaken</u>, 30 and then the sign of the Son of Man will appear in the sky, and then all the tribes of the earth will mourn, and they will see the Son of Man coming on the clouds of the sky with power and great glory. 31 "And He will send forth His angels **with a great trumpet and they will gather together His elect** from the four winds. (NAS)*

Paul says we are not meant to flee from or avoid tribulation, because it produces good things in us; i.e., perseverance, character and hope.

Rom 5:3-5 And not only this, but we also exult in our tribulations, knowing that tribulation brings about perseverance; 4 and perseverance, proven character; and proven character, hope; 5 and hope does not disappoint, because the love of God has been poured out within our hearts through the Holy Spirit who was given to us. (NAS)

Paul goes on to say that tribulation cannot separate us from the love of God. He is with us in all circumstances and uses it for our benefit. In fact, Jesus Himself showed us how to endure tribulation.

Rom 8:35-37 Who shall separate us from the love of Christ? Shall <u>tribulation, or distress, or persecution, or famine, or nakedness, or peril, or sword?</u> 36 Just as it is written, "For Thy sake we are being put to death all day long. We were considered as sheep to be

slaughtered." 37 But in all these things <u>we overwhelmingly conquer</u>
<u>through Him who loved us</u>. (NAS)

These sentiments and many others are contrary to the notion of
a Divine rescue mission from the Tribulation. Jesus told the church
at Smyrna that they would have a short period of tribulation, but that
if they would **be faithful unto death**, he would give them a crown
of life (Rev 2:10). The church will not escape the Tribulation, so we
should prepare for it by holy living and by building spiritual muscle
to withstand and to endure.

However, we will not suffer **the Wrath of God**. Tribulation is
caused by the Antichrist, the world system and by Satan. The Wrath
is caused by God and occurs at the Second Coming of Jesus. We are
not destined for Wrath.

*1 Thess 5:9-11 For **God has not destined us for wrath,** but for*
obtaining salvation through our Lord Jesus Christ, 10 who died
for us, that whether we are awake or asleep, we may live together
with Him. 11 Therefore encourage one another, and build up one
another, just as you also are doing. (NAS)

Rom 5:8-9 But God demonstrates His own love toward us, in that
while we were yet sinners, Christ died for us. 9 Much more then,
*having now been justified by His blood, **we shall be saved from***
***the wrath of God** through Him. (NAS)*

Eph 5:6 Let no one deceive you with empty words, for because of
*these things **the wrath of God comes upon the sons of disobedience**.*
(not upon God's people) (NAS)

1 Thess 1:9-10 For they themselves report about us what kind of a
reception we had with you, and how you turned to God from idols
to serve a living and true God, 10 and to wait for His Son from
*heaven, whom He raised from the dead, that is **Jesus, who delivers***
***us from the wrath to come**. (NAS)*

All of this brings us to some clear information about the timing
of the Rapture of the Church. Based on what we have seen in the

scriptures, the Rapture will occur **AFTER** the Tribulation, **BEFORE** the Wrath and **AT** the Second Coming.

Chapter 12

The Millennial Reign of Jesus Upon the Earth

THE NECESSITY OF a Millennial Reign upon the earth is embedded in **the fall of Adam and Eve in the Garden.** In His First Coming, Jesus came to cleanse us from our sins. In His Second Coming, Jesus will accomplish what the first Adam failed to do. Paul calls Adam a "metaphorical type" of Christ. This means that **we can discern what Jesus was supposed to do by understanding what Adam was given to do.**

> *Rom 5:14-15 Nevertheless death reigned from Adam until Moses, even over those who had not sinned in the likeness of the offense of **Adam, who is a type of Him who was to come**. (NAS)*

Paul also called Jesus the last Adam (1 Cor 15:45). After Jesus, there would be no other "Adams." Jesus is, in other words, the ultimate Adam. In contrast with Adam, Jesus would be obedient to the Father and not sin. In contrast with Adam, Jesus would steward the earth, ruling properly and reigning over its people to the glory of God.

Although sinful man has done and continues to do significant damage to himself and to God's creation, God's plans cannot be thwarted in the long run even by the abuse of man's free will. Isaiah tells us that **the Word of God will not fail to accomplish the purpose for which it was sent.** It is not conceivable that the Garden and Adam's calling should be a failed experiment for God just because they were failed experiences for Adam and Eve.

Isa 55:11 So shall My word be which goes forth from My mouth. It shall not return to Me empty, without accomplishing what I desire, and without succeeding in the matter for which I sent it. (NAS)

For 6,000 years evangelicals (both Jews and Christians) have expected to see the Messiah rule and reign in the earth–**a Messianic Kingdom of peace and goodness**. Some Christians believed that the Millennial Reign had already begun and was represented by the governance of the church in the earth. The expectation was that the church would eventually convert all men and cause them to become sanctified at a very high level. This theory, known as **Post-millennialism,** became harder and harder to support by actual experience over time. Most others held that the Millennial Reign was yet to come and would begin after the Second Coming of Christ. Known as **Pre-millennialism**, this has been the most prevalent theory among evangelical Christians down through the ages. It is only since the 1900s in the age of modernism that the concept of the Millennial Reign of Christ was abandoned as a literal time period. But after the worldwide "war to end all wars" was followed shortly by the second "war to end all wars," disillusioned Christians began to take all of the scriptures that had been used to describe the Millennial Reign of Christ in the earth and push them forward into "Heaven." They spiritualized obvious references to human existence as best they could and threw their lot in with a divine rescue mission in the form of a Pre-Tribulation or Mid-Tribulation Rapture. They envisioned the world in a downward spiral which not even God could fix. This theory is known as **Amillennialism**.

Modernism's poison ate away at the fabric of faith and trust in God. Christians quit preparing their children and themselves to stand and endure in the face of Satan's onslaught and began to teach them to expect a retreat to the safety of the Marriage Feast of the Lamb by means of a Pre-Trib or Mid-Trib Rapture. They abandoned God's call to holiness and its resultant spiritual authority and power in favor of popular psychology and self-help teaching. They gave the Evil One so much credit that they developed a functional dualism. In their eyes, God and Satan became equal combatants and the outcome was still hanging in the balance. God's best hope was a supernatural retreat and Jesus' best move was a rescue mission. They began to believe that the "dark side of the force" might indeed be stronger, at least in this world.

In the face of modernism and its resultant secularity, the idea of a literal Millennial Reign of Jesus upon the earth became unthinkable, even silly. And, come to think of it, so did the idea of a literal creation as described in Genesis. Academic Biblical scholars, seeking the praises of men rather than the approval of the Father, subjected the scriptures to historical criticism and joined the secularists in labeling much of the Bible as merely metaphor and myth. It had, unfortunately, been a very long time since they had actually experienced the power and presence of God. They assumed that, just because He was not speaking to them, He was, therefore, not speaking to anyone. They discounted 6,000 years of Judeo-Christian testimony as some "vast right wing conspiracy" or some monolithic, long and enduring self-delusion, as if only recently had people become intelligent or rational.

The problem is this: **If you give away the Bible at its edges (Genesis and Revelation), you will soon be fighting for it at its core.** The edges and the core are interdependent. Believe both or you will eventually believe in neither. Sure enough, today's intelligentsia are denying the virgin birth, the resurrection, the sinlessness of Jesus, His miracles, His substitutionary sacrifice for us and even the historical existence of Christ. Furthermore, they are ridiculing anyone who has the temerity to believe differently and challenging our very right to teach evangelical truth to our children.

Abraham believed God and it was credited to him as righteousness. If we believe God, we will be saved. Jesus believed in the Creation story and the Millennial Reign as did His disciples, Paul and the other writers of the New Testament. **Jesus and these others quoted the prophets as if the prophets spoke literal truth.** If we are going to trust our eternal well-being to the truth, wisdom and revelation of Jesus and His immediate followers, it would be irrational to also assume that they were unenlightened or deceived about Creation and/ or the Millennial Reign. It would also be inconsistent with belief to think that they were "winking at Heaven" when they used myths and legends while teaching the truth of the ages to unenlightened people they encountered in their day. If modern thinking were required to access God's revelation, Jesus just as easily could have been born in this age. When push comes to shove, we are "in for a penny, in for a pound."

Paul, like Isaiah, Ezekiel, John the Revelator and a few others, tells us that he has actually seen the Heaven of the hereafter (1 Cor 12 2-4). He further tells us he is not permitted to share with us the details of the heavenly realm. Finally, he tells us that **the "eye has not seen nor ear heard, neither has it entered into the heart of man" what God has laid up there for His people** (1 Cor 2:9). From that we can deduce that Heaven is a place very different from this earth and is very different in structure and experience from anything we "have ever seen or heard." Jesus tells us that the human marriage does not exist there. Our bodies have to be redesigned to exist in that realm. So what do we do with the pages and pages of references to a human existence in a peaceable kingdom with animals, birth, death, healing herbs for sick people, rivers, mountains, people who rise up in rebellion after the release of Satan from the abyss, a final battle (long after Armageddon) and so many other physical components? The answer is that we can either treat them all as allegorical and metaphorical or **we have to allow for the Millennial Reign of Christ upon the earth**.

No one is ever going to convince unbelievers that the Millennial Reign is literal nor is it the purpose of this treatise to convince unbelievers. However, evangelicals do want to see such a claim supported in scripture, and that **IS** the purpose of this writing. What follows is Biblical support for a literal Millennial Reign of Christ upon the earth in time and among humanity. Taken as a whole and in conjunction with other Biblical texts, it is compelling.

ISAIAH AND THE MILLENNIAL REIGN

The primary source of Biblical support for the Millennial Reign comes from the prophets, and the primary writing prophet of the Old Testament is Isaiah.

Isaiah 11:1-5 Then a shoot will spring from the stem of Jesse, and a branch from his roots will bear fruit. 2 And the Spirit of the LORD will rest on Him, the spirit of wisdom and understanding, the spirit of counsel and strength, the spirit of knowledge and the fear of the LORD. 3 And He will delight in the fear of the LORD. And He will not judge by what His eyes see, nor make a decision by what His ears hear; 4 but with righteousness He will judge the poor, and decide with fairness for the afflicted of the earth. And He will strike the earth with the rod of His mouth, and with the breath of His lips He will slay the wicked. 5 Also righteousness will be the belt about His loins, and faithfulness the belt about His waist. (NAS)

Here is described the Messiah, who has the seven spirits of God and yet is a son of Jesse (human). He is gentle and kind to the afflicted, a stern judge of the wicked but fair to everyone. He will rule with wisdom and spiritual insight and not be misled by just physical data. He is "rightly related" to everyone in Heaven and on the earth.

Isaiah 11:6-9 And the wolf will dwell with the lamb, and the leopard will lie down with the kid, and the calf and the young lion and the fatling together. And a little boy will lead them. 7 Also the cow and the bear will graze; their young will lie down together. And the lion will eat straw like the ox. 8 And the nursing child will play by the hole of the cobra. And the weaned child will put his hand on the viper's den. 9 They will not hurt or destroy in all My holy mountain, for the earth will be full of the knowledge of the LORD as the waters cover the sea. (NAS)

His kingdom will be a peaceable kingdom. The relationships between mankind and the animals will be like their pre-Fall relationship, without hostility or enmity. Animals will not be carnivorous any longer so that the post-Fall enemies will now dwell in peace and safety with one another. The enmity between mankind and the serpent which resulted from treachery (Genesis 3:13-15) will be undone and they will be friends again. This is an earthly kingdom, not something that is happening in Heaven. This is the Millennial Kingdom of the Messiah.

Isaiah 11:10-16 Then it will come about in that day that the nations will resort to the root of Jesse, who will stand as a signal for the peoples; and His resting place will be glorious. 11 Then it will happen on that day that the Lord will again recover the second time with His hand the remnant of His people, who will remain, from Assyria, Egypt, Pathros, Cush, Elam, Shinar, Hamath, and from the islands of the sea. 12 And He will lift up a standard for the nations, and will assemble the banished ones of Israel, and will gather the dispersed of Judah from the four corners of the earth. 13 Then the jealousy of Ephraim will depart, and those who harass Judah will be cut off. Ephraim will not be jealous of Judah, and Judah will not harass Ephraim. 14 And they will swoop down on the slopes of the Philistines on the west. Together they will plunder the sons of the east. They will possess Edom and Moab; and the sons of Ammon will be subject to them. 15 And the LORD will utterly destroy the tongue of the Sea of Egypt; and He will wave His hand over the River with His scorching wind; and He will strike it into seven streams, and make men walk over dry-shod. 16 And there will be a highway from Assyria for the remnant of His people who will be left, just as there was for Israel in the day that they came up out of the land of Egypt. (NAS)

The nations will bow down to King Jesus and He will gather all of the sons of Jacob from all over the world to come to Israel. The nations will assist in returning them to their land. The Israelites will make peace with each other. The northern kingdom of Israel and the southern kingdom of Judah will merge once again under King Jesus, the son of David. All of Israel will be restored to their land as it was given to Abraham in Genesis 17:8 and as detailed to Moses in Numbers 34:1-12. God will build a highway in the desert to allow the dispersed Israelites to walk home as at the Exodus. This is a scripture of future events that occur on the earth and is certainly not something which happens in Heaven. This is the Millennial Kingdom of Christ upon the earth.

*Isaiah 12 :1-6 Then you (**Israel**) will say on that day, "I will give thanks to Thee, O LORD. For although Thou wast angry with me, Thine anger is turned away, and Thou dost comfort me. 2 "Behold,*

*God is my salvation. I will trust and not be afraid. For the Lord
God is my strength and song, and He has become my salvation."
3 Therefore you will joyously draw water from the springs of
salvation. 4 And in that day you will say, "Give thanks to the LORD,
call on His name. Make known His deeds among the peoples; make
them remember that His name is exalted." 5 Praise the LORD in
song, for He has done excellent things. Let this be known throughout
the earth. 6 Cry aloud and shout for joy, O inhabitant of Zion, for
great in your midst is the Holy One of Israel. (NAS)*

The Jews will rejoice in that day and recognize their Messiah.
They will understand that salvation comes from relationship with God
and not from keeping the Law. They will learn what Abraham knew
and what Jesus and Paul tried to teach them in the first century.

*Isa 65:17-20 "For behold, I create new heavens and a new earth;
and the former things shall not be remembered or come to mind.
18 "But be glad and rejoice forever in what I create. For behold, I
create Jerusalem for rejoicing, and her people for gladness. 19 "I
will also rejoice in Jerusalem, and be glad in My people. And there
will no longer be heard in her the voice of weeping and the sound
of crying. 20 "No longer will there be in it an infant who lives but
a few days, or an old man who does not live out his days; for the
youth will die at the age of one hundred and the one who does not
reach the age of one hundred shall be thought accursed. (NAS)*

After the cataclysmic return of Christ accompanied by earthquakes, asteroids, fires and general destruction, God will create a
new earth and new heavens above it. Jerusalem will be restored and
God's people, the Jews, will dwell in it and be glad. There will not be
weeping or premature death. Living only 100 years is seen as having
died as a child and accursed. Here we are seeing the long lives of the
people before the Fall and probably for the same reason. God will
have restored the "rachiya" and the canopy will again be in place.
God's original plan of Creation will once more be in place with a
new Adam whose name is Jesus (1 Cor 15). The Garden has been
restored. The brilliance of God's plan will now be demonstrated on

the earth. His word does not go out and return to Him void without having accomplished its task (Is 55:11).

> *Isa 65: 21-25 "And they shall build houses and inhabit them. They shall also plant vineyards and eat their fruit. 22 "They shall not build, and another inhabit. They shall not plant, and another eat; for as the lifetime of a tree, so shall be the days of My people, and My chosen ones shall wear out the work of their hands. 23 "They shall not labor in vain, or bear children for calamity; for they are the offspring of those blessed by the LORD, and their descendants with them. 24 "It will also come to pass that before they call, I will answer; and while they are still speaking, I will hear. 25 "The wolf and the lamb shall graze together, and the lion shall eat straw like the ox; and dust shall be the serpent's food. They shall do no evil or harm in all My holy mountain," says the LORD.*

This is a realm of normal human existence, not a spiritual realm. It is not Heaven. People are building houses, planting crops, having children and calling on the name of the Lord for assistance. The animals will no longer be carnivorous. They who have been mortal enemies will dwell in peace with each other. (Apparently the hippies had it right. We are meant to get back to the Garden. ☺)

JEREMIAH AND THE MILLENNIAL REIGN

> *Jer 3:14-19 'Return, O faithless sons,' declares the LORD; 'for I am a master to you, and I will take you one from a city and two from a family, and I will bring you to Zion.' "Then I will give you shepherds after My own heart, who will feed you on knowledge and understanding." And it shall be in those days when you are multiplied and increased in the land," declares the LORD, "they shall say no more, 'The ark of the covenant of the LORD.' And it shall not come to mind, nor shall they remember it, nor shall they miss {it,} nor shall it be made again. "At that time they shall call Jerusalem 'the Throne of the LORD,' and all the nations will be gathered to it, to Jerusalem, for the name of the LORD. Nor shall they walk anymore after the stubbornness of their evil heart." In those days the house of Judah will walk with the house of Israel, and they will come together from the land of the north to the land*

that I gave your fathers as an inheritance. "Then I said, 'How I would set you among My sons, and give you a pleasant land, the most beautiful inheritance of the nations!' And I said, 'You shall call me, My Father, and not turn away from following me.' (NAS)

Jeremiah also predicts that God will gather His sons from all over the globe to return them to Israel. He will give them good pastors who will teach them correctly. The Ark of the Covenant which had been a metaphorical type or symbol of God's presence will not be remade, because God will dwell personally with His people in Jerusalem. Israel will multiply and prosper. They will be faithful to the Lord and will dwell peacefully with one another. The schism between Judah and the ten northern tribes will be healed.

EZEKIEL AND THE MILLENNIAL REIGN

Ezek 47:1-2 Then he brought me back to the door of the house; and behold, water was flowing from under the threshold of the house toward the east, for the house faced east. And the water was flowing down from under, from the right side of the house, from south of the altar. 2 And he brought me out by way of the north gate and led me around on the outside to the outer gate by way of the gate that faces east. And behold, water was trickling from the south side. 3 When the man went out toward the east with a line in his hand, he measured a thousand cubits, and he led me through the water, water reaching the ankles. 4 Again he measured a thousand and led me through the water, water reaching the knees. Again he measured a thousand and led me through the water, water reaching the loins. 5 Again he measured a thousand; and it was a river that I could not ford, for the water had risen, enough water to swim in, a river that could not be forded. 6 And he said to me, "Son of man, have you seen this?"

A river will flow from under the throne from south to east. As it leaves the city, it grows deeper and deeper until it can no longer be forded.

Ezek 47:7-12 Then he brought me back to the bank of the river. 7 Now when I had returned, behold, on the bank of the river there were very many trees on the one side and on the other. 8 Then he said to me, "These waters go out toward the eastern region and go down into the Arabah; then they go toward the sea, being made to flow into the sea, and the waters of the sea become fresh. 9 "And it will come about that every living creature which swarms in every place where the river goes, will live. And there will be very many fish, for these waters go there, and the others become fresh; so everything will live where the river goes. 10 "And it will come about that fishermen will stand beside it; from Engedi to Eneglaim there will be a place for the spreading of nets. Their fish will be according to their kinds, like the fish of the Great Sea, very many.

Trees will grow up on both banks of the river. This will be in stark contrast to the prior lack of trees caused by a history of an increasingly toxic, poorly stewarded environment and by the cataclysms associated with Jesus' return. The water from the throne also will cause the sea water to become fresh. Everywhere the river flows, there is healing and restoration in the earth. Fish once again teem in the waters. Fishermen shall catch many fish. The Garden is being restored.

11 "But its swamps and marshes will not become fresh; they will be left for salt. 12 "And by the river on its bank, on one side and on the other, will grow all kinds of trees for food. Their leaves will not wither, and their fruit will not fail. They will bear every month because their water flows from the sanctuary, and their fruit will be for food and their leaves for healing." (NAS)

Swamps and marshes will continue to be salt water. Fruit-bearing trees will grow up along the river banks to be useful for food. Their fruit will bear monthly all year round. The leaves of these trees will be useful for healing. Once again, this is human existence on the earth after the coming of the Lord.

ZECHARIAH AND THE MILLENNIAL REIGN

Zech 14:1-3 Behold, a day is coming for the LORD when the spoil taken from you will be divided among you. 2 For I will gather all the nations against Jerusalem to battle. And the city will be captured, the houses plundered, the women ravished, and half of the city exiled, but the rest of the people will not be cut off from the city. 3 Then the LORD will go forth and fight against those nations, as when He fights on a day of battle.

Zechariah promised Israel that they would have restored all of the spoils of battle that had been plundered from them. The nations of the earth had been cruel and unjust towards God's people. God will lure nations up to Jerusalem to punish God's people, but then He will go forth as a warrior on the side of the Jews.

Zech 14:4-5 4 And in that day His feet will stand on the Mount of Olives, which is in front of Jerusalem on the east; and the Mount of Olives will be split in its middle from east to west by a very large valley, so that half of the mountain will move toward the north and the other half toward the south. 5 And you will flee by the valley of My mountains, for the valley of the mountains will reach to Azel. Yes, you will flee just as you fled before the earthquake in the days of Uzziah king of Judah.

When Jesus returns and touches down on the Mount of Olives, the great earthquake predicted previously shall occur. Mountains will fall into the sea and the valleys will be raised up so a highway can be forged in the desert for all people to return to God and to one another. Sin creates barriers and the undoing of sin undoes those barriers. The people of God will scramble so as not to get caught up in this geophysical event. For additional scriptures on these events, see Appendix III–The Themes of Isaiah.

Then the LORD, my God, will come, and all the holy ones with Him! 6 And it will come about in that day that there will be no light; the luminaries will dwindle. 7 For it will be a unique day which is known to the LORD, neither day nor night, but it will come about that at evening time there will be light. (see also Rev 21:23-25 and 22:5) 8 And it will come about in that day that living waters will flow out of Jerusalem, half of them toward the eastern sea and the other half toward the western sea; it will be in summer as well as in winter. (NAS)

This will happen in conjunction with the Second Coming. The sun and the stars will fall out of the sky, but God's people will be sustained by the light of God as on the First Day of Creation. There will no longer be "day and night" as such, but it will always be daytime. Once again we are told about the waters flowing from Jerusalem. Once again we see the restoration of the Garden as in the beginning.

Zech 14:9-11 And the LORD will be king over all the earth. In that day the LORD will be the only one, and His name the only one. 10 All the land will be changed into a plain from Geba to Rimmon south of Jerusalem; but Jerusalem will rise and remain on its site from Benjamin's Gate as far as the place of the First Gate to the Corner Gate, and from the Tower of Hananel to the king's wine presses. 11 And people will live in it, and there will be no more curse, for Jerusalem will dwell in security. (NAS)

Jesus will reign in the earth as King and Jerusalem shall be lifted up as the highest city on the earth. The people who live there will have security and blessings.

Zech 14:12-15 Now this will be the plague with which the LORD will strike all the peoples who have gone to war against Jerusalem. Their flesh will rot while they stand on their feet, and their eyes will rot in their sockets, and their tongue will rot in their mouth. 13 And it will come about in that day that a great panic from the LORD will fall on them; and they will seize one another's hand, and the hand of one will be lifted against the hand of another. 14 And Judah also will fight at Jerusalem; and the wealth of all the surrounding nations will be gathered, gold and silver and garments in great abundance. 15 So also like this plague, will be the plague on the horse, the mule, the camel, the donkey, and all the cattle that will be in those camps.

The Lord will strike Israel's enemies with a plague of rotting flesh, rotting eyes and a rotting tongue. The enemies of the Lord will begin to kill each other in the confusion and fog of war. Their military transport (horses, mules, etc,) will also be killed rendering them helpless to fight or flee from Israel's wrath. Israel will despoil them in repayment for past persecutions.

> *Zech 14:16-19 Then it will come about that any who are left of all the nations that went against Jerusalem will go up from year to year to worship the King, the LORD of hosts, and to celebrate the Feast of Booths. 17 And it will be that whichever of the families of the earth does not go up to Jerusalem to worship the King, the LORD of hosts, there will be no rain on them. 18 And if the family of Egypt does not go up or enter, then no rain will fall on them. It will be the plague with which the LORD smites the nations who do not go up to celebrate the Feast of Booths. 19 This will be the punishment of Egypt, and the punishment of all the nations who do not go up to celebrate the Feast of Booths.*

Israel's enemies will bow down before Israel's King and go up to Jerusalem for the Jewish feasts. Should they fail to go up to Jerusalem to honor God during the Feasts, they will be punished by plague and pestilence.

> *20 In that day there will be inscribed on the bells of the horses, "HOLY TO THE LORD." And the cooking pots in the Lord's house will be like the bowls before the altar. 21 And every cooking pot in Jerusalem and in Judah will be holy to the LORD of hosts; and all who sacrifice will come and take of them and boil in them. And there will no longer be a Canaanite in the house of the LORD of hosts in that day.* (NAS)

The decorative bells on their coaches (modern bumper stickers ☺?) will sport verbiage praising God. Everyone will eat clean food and offer thanks to God for each meal. Here again is human existence in the earth after the return of Christ.

JOHN THE REVELATOR AND THE MILLENNIAL REIGN

> *Rev 5:9-10 And they sang a new song, saying, "Worthy art Thou to take the book, and to break its seals; for Thou wast slain, and didst purchase for God with Thy blood {men} from every tribe and*

tongue and people and nation." And **Thou hast made them {to be}** **a kingdom and priests to our God; and they will reign upon** **the** **earth**. *" (NAS)*

God's people will become a nation of priests and kings in the earth, ministering to all nations. God's people will rule and reign on the earth.

Rev 21:1-8 And I saw a new heaven and a new earth; for the first heaven and the first earth passed away, and there is no longer any sea. 2 And I saw the holy city, new Jerusalem, coming down out of heaven from God, made ready as a bride adorned for her husband. (NAS)

John the Revelator also sees the new heaven and new earth. He also tells about the Holy City coming down out of Heaven. He compares "her" to a bride about to receive a husband.

3 And I heard a loud voice from the throne, saying, "Behold, the tabernacle of God is among men, and He shall dwell among them, and they shall be His people, and God Himself shall be among them, 4 and He shall wipe away every tear from their eyes; and there shall no longer be any death; there shall no longer be any mourning, or crying, or pain; the first things have passed away." 5 And He who sits on the throne said, "Behold, I am making all things new." And He said, "Write, for these words are faithful and true." 6 And He said to me, "It is done. I am the Alpha and the Omega, the beginning and the end. I will give to the one who thirsts from the spring of the water of life without cost. 7 "He who overcomes shall inherit these things, and I will be his God and he will be My son. 8 "But for the cowardly and unbelieving and abominable and murderers and immoral persons and sorcerers and idolaters and all liars, their part will be in the lake that burns with fire and brimstone, which is the second death." (NAS)

Heaven will bear witness to the phenomenon—God is going to dwell among His people. God's people will not die or have sorrow any longer. All things are being restored (making them new). If anyone is faithful until then, he will be included in the glory. It will come to the faithful (the believers) with no cost to them. They shall be called the "sons" of God. However, those who dwelt in fear, lacking faith, having given themselves to false gods, having sought the wisdom of demons along with murderers, sorcerers and immoral persons will go to Hell, the Lake of Fire, also known as the Second Death.

Rev 21:9-21 And one of the seven angels who had the seven bowls full of the seven last plagues, came and spoke with me, saying, "Come here, I shall show you the bride, the wife of the Lamb." 10 And he carried me away in the Spirit to a great and high mountain, and showed me the holy city, Jerusalem, coming down out of heaven from God, 11 having the glory of God. Her brilliance was like a very costly stone, as a stone of crystal-clear jasper. 12 It had a great and high wall, with twelve gates, and at the gates twelve angels; and names were written on them, which are those of the twelve tribes of the sons of Israel. 13 There were three gates on the east and three gates on the north and three gates on the south and three gates on the west. 14 And the wall of the city had twelve foundation stones, and on them were the twelve names of the twelve apostles of the Lamb. 15 And the one who spoke with me had a gold measuring rod to measure the city, and its gates and its wall. 16 And the city is laid out as a square, and its length is as great as the width; and he measured the city with the rod, fifteen hundred miles; its length and width and height are equal. 17 And he measured its wall, seventy-two yards, according to human measurements, which are also angelic measurements. 18 And the material of the wall was jasper; and the city was pure gold, like clear glass. 19 The foundation stones of the city wall were adorned with every kind of precious stone. The first foundation stone was jasper; the second, sapphire; the third, chalcedony; the fourth, emerald; 20 the fifth, sardonyx; the sixth, sardius; the seventh, chrysolite; the eighth, beryl; the ninth, topaz; the tenth, chrysoprase; the eleventh, jacinth; the twelfth, amethyst. 21; each one of the gates was a single pearl. And the street of the city was pure gold, like transparent glass. (NAS)

This picture of the New Jerusalem coming down from out of Heaven to be located on the New Earth is one of the most enduring images of the Eschaton. It shows up in a number of Biblical passages, the writings of the church fathers, the writings of the reformers and no small number of hymns. Prominently featured are its "pearly gates." That this was an earthly city in a human world was never in doubt until modern times. Taken in context with all other Millennial Reign scriptures, it is clearly seen to exist in time and space on our earth. However, in the age of Modernism (roughly 1850-1970) it was just too much to swallow for the scientific mind. Having dispensed with the Virgin Birth, the resurrection of Jesus from the dead, the divinity of Christ and all miracles, liberal theologians easily tossed this image into the realm of "Heaven" which they often spoke of as allegorical and metaphorical at best.

> *Rev21:22-27 And I saw no temple in it, for the Lord God, the Almighty, and the Lamb, are its temple. 23 And the city has no need of the sun or of the moon to shine upon it, for the glory of God has illumined it, and its lamp is the Lamb. 24 And the nations shall walk by its light, and the kings of the earth shall bring their glory into it. 25 And in the daytime (for there shall be no night there) its gates shall never be closed; 26 and they shall bring the glory and the honor of the nations into it; 27 and nothing unclean and no one who practices abomination and lying, shall ever come into it, but only those whose names are written in the Lamb's book of life. (NAS)*

We are told that the temple, which had been a metaphorical type of God's presence among us, is no longer necessary, because God will actually be residing among us in the human form of King Jesus. There will be no need of a sun because Jesus will provide light to the world by God's presence as He did in the First Day of Creation (Gen 1:3-5), only this time, there will be no darkness in the New Jerusalem. The born again saints will come and go there at will. The unregenerate will only be able to see it from afar, but see it they will.

> *Revelation 22:1 And he showed me a river of the water of life, clear as crystal, coming from the throne of God and of the Lamb, 2 in*

the middle of its street. And on either side of the river was the tree of life, bearing twelve kinds of fruit, yielding its fruit every month; and the leaves of the tree were for the healing of the nations. 3 And there shall no longer be any curse; and the throne of God and of the Lamb shall be in it, and His bond-servants shall serve Him; 4 and they shall see His face, and His name shall be on their foreheads. 5 And there shall no longer be any night; and they shall not have need of the light of a lamp nor the light of the sun, because the Lord God shall illumine them; and they shall reign forever and ever. (NAS)

From under the throne of Jesus will flow the River of Life. It will cause fruit-bearing trees to grow up on its banks producing fruit 12 months of the year for food, reminiscent of the Lord's provision of food in the desert for 40 years for a wandering Israel. The leaves of these trees will be good for healing those who become ill among the nations. A true Heaven would have neither the ailing nor the unsaved nations residing in its midst. Along with all of the other scriptures about this age, we are given a solid picture of human existence on the earth. We see an earth ruled by Jesus the King and his born again servants, "a nation of kings and priests unto our God." We see the Millennial Reign of Christ upon the earth.

Evangelicals in every age in both Judaic and Christian theology have refused to throw out the literal and physical nature of scriptural references like these. In the face of withering scorn and pseudo-scientific thinking, some evangelicals retreated from the Genesis account and the eschatological scriptures, including the book of Revelation, in hopes of saving the Bible at its core; i.e., the Virgin Birth, the Resurrection, the Divinity of Christ and His physical return to the earth. But they eventually found out that if you give away the Bible at its edges, you will soon be struggling to protect its center. Treating Genesis and the Eschaton as allegories leads inevitably to reducing the Virgin Birth and the Resurrection to allegories. There is no need to surrender either Genesis or Revelation. They should both be held as solidly as the Virgin Birth and the Resurrection. They all require the same level of faith.

Chapter 13

The Great White Throne Judgment–the Sheep versus the Goats

IN ORDER TO properly frame the Great White Throne Judgment, I am going to repeat some comments from earlier chapters. Please bear with me.

Every man must die and face the Judge of all the earth to account for his sins. The Bible speaks against reincarnation. Each person dies one time and then comes to judgment (Heb 9:27).

The <u>righteous dead</u> go immediately into the presence of God at the moment of their death and, more importantly, into the presence of Jesus, the Christ. All of us are found guilty of sin, but those of us who have our names written into the Lamb's Book of Life will not be judged according to our deeds, but according to Jesus' righteousness. Satan accuses us to God and justifiably so. But Jesus imparts His righteousness to us. He gives us His bloodstained cloak through which God cannot see our sins. His righteousness not only is imparted to us (**given as a gift**) but is imputed to us. Imputation means we are justified, that is, treated "<u>just as if I'd</u>" not sinned. The blood of Jesus causes us to become like Him, and God will "remember our sins no more" (Heb 8:12).

As we outlined earlier, the unrighteous dead go to Sheol where they "sleep" until the end of time. Sheol is the Old Testament place of the dead. It is sometimes in the scriptures referred to as a prison, a pit, the grave or a place of sleep or mindless dreaming. The Greek name for it is "Hades" (not to be confused with Hell which is another place altogether) (Ps 146:2-4).

Death as a condition of sleep or mindless dreaming is not received by all believers over time, so an explanation with Biblical support is offered earlier in the section entitled Soul Sleep (see the index). It is reiterated briefly at this point in order to illuminate the Great White Throne judgment.

Sleep as a euphemism for death is common in both the Old and New Testaments. Job complains to God that if God allows him to go down into Sheol, he (Job) will not be capable of praising God. The theology of Job and most other Old Testament men and women held that there was no conscious moment in the grave (Job 14:10-14).

The timing of the final judgment is indicated here. The dead will rise up out of their sleep "when the heavens be no more." He is speaking of the unrighteous dead asleep in Sheol. About them, he is absolutely correct. For all of Job's knowledge of God, he is not able to see the events of the death and resurrection of Jesus and His despoiling of Sheol. However, Job's high theology expects an afterlife somehow and sometime after Sheol (Eccl 9:5-11).

Solomon believed in "soul sleep," reflecting the firmly held belief of all of the men and women of his day.

*Dan 12:2-3 "And many of those **who sleep in the dust of the ground** will awake, these to everlasting life, but the others to disgrace and everlasting contempt. (NAS)*

Daniel has the Great White Throne Judgment in view here–a day of judgment when all the dead will arise and be separated as between "sheep and goats."

*Matt 27:49-53...and Jesus cried out again with a loud voice, and yielded up His spirit. 51 And behold, the veil of the temple was torn in two from top to bottom, and the earth shook; and the rocks were split, 52 **and the tombs were opened; and many bodies of the saints who had fallen asleep were raised; 53 and coming out of the tombs after His resurrection they entered the holy city and appeared to many**. (NAS)*

Here we see the righteous dead of the Old Testament being awakened and taken to Heaven at the time of Jesus' death and resurrection (the despoiling of Sheol). This group and all subsequent believers go straight to God to be judged upon their death. As Paul tells us, to be absent the body (for a believer) is to be present with Christ. This leaves only the unrighteous dead left asleep in Sheol. They are awakened for judgment at the end of time, at the end of the Millennial Reign "when the heavens be no more;" that is, at the Great White Throne judgment.

> *1 Cor 15:16-26 For if the dead are not raised, not even Christ has been raised; 17 and if Christ has not been raised, your faith is worthless; you are still in your sins. 18* ***Then those also who have fallen asleep in Christ have perished*.** *19 If we have hoped in Christ in this life only, we are of all men most to be pitied. 20 But* **now *Christ has been raised from the dead, the first fruits of those who are asleep*.** *21 For since by a man came death, by a man also came the resurrection of the dead. 22 For as in Adam all die, so also in Christ all shall be made alive. 23 But each in his own order: Christ the first fruits, after that those who are Christ's at His coming, 24 then comes the end, when He delivers up the kingdom to the God and Father, when He has abolished all rule and all authority and power. 25 For He must reign until He has put all His enemies under His feet. 26 The last enemy that will be abolished is death. (NAS)*

Here we see the timing for several events.
- First we see Jesus resurrected in His glorified body on Easter Sunday.
- Next we see the righteous dead resurrected in their glorified bodies at the Second Coming of Christ.
- Then we see the Millennial Reign in which Jesus reigns "until He has put all of His enemies under His feet." The conquering of death places the end of the Millennial Reign squarely in human time. This means that the Millennial Reign is an event that occurs in time and space, not in Heaven or the hereafter as some have claimed.
- Finally, we see Jesus hand the kingdom to His Father in Heaven. He has then accomplished all He was sent to do.

David and Isaiah also describe Sheol as a vague dream state or a place of unconsciousness (Ps 6:4-6; 31:17; Is 38:18).

So what is the Great White Throne Judgment? At the end of the Millennial Reign of Christ on the earth (about 1000 years after the Second Coming) a judgment will occur at which time all of the souls of the unrighteous dead will be awakened in Sheol and brought before the Lord for sentencing along with the good and the evil people who lived during the Millennial Reign. This is known as the Great White Throne Judgment (see below). The righteous dead, having already been judged when they died and having ruled and reigned with Christ for 1000 years, will be witnesses. The righteous living at the time of this Great White Throne judgment will be judged and make up the group referred to in Matthew 25: 31-46 as the sheep. After this judgment in which Death and Hades give up their prisoners (inhabitants), the souls of the unrighteous dead (the goats in Matthew 25:31-46) will all go into Hell, the Lake of Fire, to join the Antichrist and the False Prophet, the first two residents of Hell, who had inaugurated it 1000 years earlier at the Second Coming. The Bible describes this event partially in Revelation 20:7-15 and partially in Matthew 25:31-46.

Rev 20:7-10 And when the thousand years are completed, Satan will be released from his prison, 8 and will come out to deceive the nations which are in the four corners of the earth, Gog and Magog, to gather them together for the war; the number of them is like the sand of the seashore. 9 And they came up on the broad plain of the earth and surrounded the camp of the saints and the beloved city, and fire came down from heaven and devoured them. 10 And the devil who deceived them was thrown into the lake of fire and brimstone, where the beast and the false prophet are also; and they will be tormented day and night forever and ever. (NAS)

At the end of the Millennial Reign, Satan is released, gathers his followers and makes a brief and unsuccessful war on Jesus and His followers. It is the last desperate act of Satan to gain the kingdom he has sought from before time. It results in his ultimate demise and the clear separation of his followers from those who belong to God in Christ.

*Rev 20:11-13 11 And I saw a **great white throne** and Him who sat upon it, from whose presence <u>earth and heaven fled away</u>, and no place was found for them. 12 And I saw the dead, the great and the small, standing before the throne, and books were opened; and another book was opened, which is the book of life; and the dead were judged from the things which were written in the books, according to their deeds. 13 <u>And the sea gave up the dead which were in it, and death and Hades gave up the dead which were in them; and they were judged, every one of them according to their deeds.</u> (NAS)*

Any who have previously been judged will not participate in this judgment. These include the righteous dead of the Old Testament whom Jesus took to Heaven at His resurrection (the despoiling of Sheol), any believer who has died since that time and the raptured saints at His Second Coming.

All others who have not been judged previously will be judged here. This includes the unrighteous dead in Sheol from all time and the people (both good and bad) who live during the Millennial Reign and are still alive at this time.

<u>14 And death and Hades</u> were thrown into the lake of fire. This is the second death, the lake of fire. 15 And if anyone's name was not found written in the book of life, he was thrown into the lake of fire. (NAS)

At this time, Hades (Sheol) is emptied and dispensed with forever. Physical death will never occur again and it, too, is "thrown into the Lake of Fire". In other words, no one will ever die again. From this point on, all creatures (angels and mankind) will either dwell in the presence of God (Heaven) or dwell in eternal separation from God (the second death, the Lake of Fire or Hell).

Jesus Himself describes this Great White Throne Judgment in Matthew 25. His description of it has usually been called "<u>the judgment of the sheep and the goats.</u>" From here we gain an understanding of the basis of the Great White Throne Judgment. Paul tells us that <u>all salvation is based in relationship and all real relationship is based</u>

in trust or faith. Abraham believed God and it was counted to him as righteousness (Gen 15:6; Rom 4:3-9, 19-24; Gal 3:6; Jas 2:23; Ps 106:31). All believers are judged on the basis of their relationship with Jesus "and not by works lest any man should boast."

Those who do not have a relationship with Jesus will have to be judged based on their deeds, their works, their behaviors, the keeping of the commandments. The two great commandments from which all others are derived are "Love God" and "Love your neighbor." It is on this basis that men are justified or condemned according to Jesus in Matthew 25.

> *Matt 25:31-33 "But when the Son of Man comes in His glory, and all the angels with Him, then He will sit on His glorious throne. 32 "And all the nations will be gathered before Him; and He will separate them from one another, as the shepherd separates the sheep from the goats; 33 and He will put the sheep on His right, and the goats on the left. (NAS)*

At the end of the Millennial Reign, all those who have not yet been judged (whether dead or alive) will be judged in preparation for the assignment of all people to either Heaven or Hell. As we have seen previously, the heavens will at this time "be no more." Jesus will have reigned on the earth for 1,000 years during which Satan will have been bound and people will have lived in the earthly kingdom of God since the return of Jesus–The Messiah of the Jews. Satan's release at the end of that period of time will force all men and women upon the earth to choose sides. It is this group that is largely in view in Jesus' teaching in Matthew 25. The unrighteous dead would quickly be dispensed with. Lacking the saving relationship with Christ, they would be judged on their deeds and found wanting. Their fate is more clearly seen in Revelation 20:13. The purpose of Jesus' teaching in Matthew 25:31-46 is to discuss the fate of those who are alive at the end of the Millennial Kingdom, particularly the Gentiles. The context of His statements is a sermon, known as the Olivet Discourse, in which He is talking about the Eschaton (end times or last days) and how it relates to Israel in particular.

Matt 25:34-36 34 "Then the King will say to those on His right, 'Come, you who are blessed of My Father, inherit the kingdom prepared for you from the foundation of the world. 35 'For I was hungry, and you gave Me something to eat; I was thirsty, and you gave Me drink; I was a stranger, and you invited Me in; 36 naked, and you clothed Me; I was sick, and you visited Me; I was in prison, and you came to Me.' (NAS)

The basis of their salvation is whether or not they related rightly to Jesus. How did they treat Him when they encountered Him? Did they love God (Jesus) and did they love their neighbor (a representative of Jesus)? All salvation is based in relationship. In the Bible, the term for right relationship is "righteousness." If while they were alive they did relate rightly to Jesus, they are His "sheep" and may enter into the joy of their Master.

Matt 25:37-40 "Then the righteous will answer Him, saying, 'Lord, when did we see You hungry, and feed You, or thirsty, and give You drink? 38' And when did we see You a stranger, and invite You in, or naked, and clothe You? 39' And when did we see You sick, or in prison, and come to You?' 40 "And the King will answer and say to them, 'Truly I say to you, to the extent that you did it to one of these brothers of Mine, even the least of them, you did it to Me.' (NAS)

Many of the righteous are surprised by their selection because they do not remember ever showing these kindnesses to Jesus. However, Jesus tells them that when they "did it to the least of these my brethren, you did it unto Me." The "brethren" referenced here is specifically Israel. By extrapolation, it can be applied to all of God's people, but that is not its contextual meaning. These words are spoken by Jesus to His Jewish followers on the Mount of Olives in a sermon known as the Olivet Discourse. It is addressed specifically to the Jews who have rejected His ministry and are about to crucify Him. Therefore, the context of the Olivet Discourse (Mt 21:18–25:46) tells us that this scripture concerning "My brethren" is about Israelites (and how the Gentiles have treated them).

A closer look at the Olivet Discourse will make this clear. The Olivet Discourse follows on the heels of His triumphal entry into

Jerusalem in which the Jews acknowledge Jesus as the Messiah on Palm Sunday but reject Him five days later on Good Friday. It speaks about the cleansing of the temple (Israel), the cursing of the fig tree (Israel), the parable of the two sons (obedience vs. religion), the parable of the landowner (Israel's rejection of God's authority and God's Son), the parable of the Marriage Feast (same theme–second telling for effect), the conflicts with the Jewish leaders (the Pharisees, the Herodians and the Sadducees), the two great commandments (the basis of judgment), Jesus' lament over Jerusalem, the prophecies concerning the destruction of the temple, the tribulation, the Second Coming, the second reference to the fig tree (Israel), the reference to the days of Noah, the illustration of the two servants (again obedience vs. religion), the parables of the virgins and the talents (mainly about the judgment of Israel) and then the judgment of the Gentiles here in our scripture. The words of Matthew 25: 31-46 are spoken at the end of Jesus' last-ditch effort to warn Israel that their rejection of Him will result in God's rejection of them. However, it also promises retribution on all those who fail to treat Israel righteously and an end time restoration of their relationship to God.

The location of this judgment at the end of all things (vv. 31-32) tells us that this is a part of the Great White Throne Judgment in Revelation, chapter 20.

Matt 25:41-46 "Then He will also say to those on His left, 'Depart from Me, accursed ones, into the eternal fire which has been prepared for the devil and his angels; 42 for I was hungry, and you gave Me nothing to eat; I was thirsty, and you gave Me nothing to drink; 43 I was a stranger, and you did not invite Me in; naked, and you did not clothe Me; sick, and in prison, and you did not visit Me.' 44 "Then they themselves also will answer, saying, 'Lord, when did we see You hungry, or thirsty, or a stranger, or naked, or sick, or in prison, and did not take care of You?' 45 "Then He will answer them, saying, 'Truly I say to you, to the extent that you did not do it to one of the least of these, you did not do it to Me.' 46 "And these will go away into eternal punishment, but the righteous into eternal life." (NAS)

Once again, there are many on the left who are surprised that they are damned. They are probably good people in their own eyes. Maybe they are churchgoers. Maybe they are relatively righteous in their behaviors. Perhaps they have measured up to the standards they imagined that would get them saved. They may have given tithes and alms and kept the commandments (for the most part). However, they missed the one standard by which God would judge them–relationship with Jesus. Had they encountered Jesus, they would have treated Him with great respect and care, but they do not remember ever personally encountering Him.

Jesus tells them that although they may have never mistreated Him personally, they were required to show their love of God by loving "the least of these, My brethren–their neighbor. Once again both context and location points to their treatment of Jews. Jesus tells them that when "you did it to the least of these my brethren, you did it unto Me." The brethren referenced here is specifically Israel. By extrapolation, it can be applied to all of God's people, but that is not its contextual meaning.

Remember: in the Millennial Reign we have a Jewish King ruling in the earth and a preeminent Israel established as prophetically promised. It is for literal Israel that the Messiah returned to conquer the nations abusing her. They are the natural branch grafted back in as Paul tells us in Rom 11:17-24. The age of the Gentile is over and we have just come through the last seven years of Daniel's prophecy; i.e. the Tribulation. Israel, not the Gentile church, is the focus. God's promises to Abraham are in view.

Chapter 14

The End of Time and of the World and the Beginning of "Heaven"

THE ULTIMATE END of the earth occurs after the Millennial Reign when the earth and the heavens are consumed by fire.

2 Peter 3:2-7 Know this first of all, that in the last days mockers will come with their mocking, following after their own lusts, 4 and saying, "Where is the promise of His coming? For ever since the fathers fell asleep, all continues just as it was from the beginning of creation." 5 For when they maintain this, it escapes their notice that by the word of God the heavens existed long ago and the earth was formed out of water and by water, 6 through which the world at that time was destroyed, being flooded with water. 7 But the present heavens and earth by His word are being reserved for fire, kept for the day of judgment and destruction of ungodly men. (NAS)

2 Peter 3:8-11 But do not let this one fact escape your notice, beloved, that with the Lord one day is as a thousand years, and a thousand years as one day. 9 The Lord is not slow about His promise, as some count slowness, but is patient toward you, not wishing for any to perish but for all to come to repentance. 10 But the day of the Lord will come like a thief, in which the heavens will pass away with a roar and the elements will be destroyed with intense heat, and the earth and its works will be burned up. (NAS)

Once we put the Millennial Reign scriptures into the Eschaton where they belong and take them out of "Heaven" where they have been erroneously misplaced by many in recent years, we find that there is little that we know about Heaven itself.

Paul says about Heaven that "eye has not seen and ear has not heard, and which have not entered the heart of man, all that God has prepared for those who love Him." He also tells us he has seen Heaven but is not permitted to describe much of it.

2 Cor 12:2-4 I know a man in Christ who fourteen years ago– whether in the body I do not know, or out of the body I do not know, God knows– such a man was caught up to the third heaven. 3 And I know how such a man– whether in the body or apart from the body I do not know, God knows– 4 was caught up into Paradise, and heard inexpressible words, which a man is not permitted to speak. (NAS)

THE THRONE OF GOD AND HIS CHRIST

One thing that we know about Heaven is that it contains the throne room of God. Several prophets have been given a vision of it and Jesus verifies this point in Mt 5:34. Their descriptions of God's throne are consistent with one another in many ways and may indeed be literal. Or they may be metaphorical. In either case, they reveal a very different world than the Millennial Reign scriptures describe.

Isa 6:1-8 In the year of King, Uzziah's death, I saw the Lord sitting on a throne, lofty and exalted, with the train of His robe filling the temple. 2 Seraphim stood above Him, each having six wings; with two he covered his face, and with two he covered his feet, and with two he flew. 3 And one called out to another and said, "Holy, Holy, Holy, is the LORD of hosts, the whole earth is full of His glory." 4 And the foundations of the thresholds trembled at the voice of him who called out, while the temple was filling with smoke. 5 Then I said, "Woe is me, for I am ruined!, Because I am a man of unclean lips, And I live among a people of unclean lips; For my eyes have seen the King, the LORD of hosts." 6 Then one of the seraphim flew to me, with a burning coal in his hand which he had taken from the altar with tongs. 7 And he touched my mouth with it and said, "Behold, this has touched your lips; and your iniquity is taken away, and your sin is forgiven." 8 Then I heard the voice of the Lord, saying, "Whom shall I send, and who will go for Us?" Then I said, "Here am I. Send me!" (NAS)

The throne room of God is a place of holiness and of judgment. Spirit beings of all kinds approach it, but no one enters there who is corrupted. <u>We are told it is located in Heaven</u>.

Job 1:6 Now there was a day when the sons of God came to present themselves before the LORD, and Satan also came among them. (NAS)

Job 2:1 Again there was a day when the sons of God came to present themselves before the LORD, and Satan also came among them to present himself before the LORD. (NAS)

Ps 11:4 The LORD is in His holy temple; <u>the Lord's throne is in heaven;</u> (NAS)

Ps 103:19 The LORD has <u>established His throne in the heavens;</u> and His sovereignty rules over all. (NAS)

Stephen in Acts 7:49 and Jesus in Mt 5:34 both quote Isaiah 66:1 in this matter when Isaiah, speaking for God, says: "Thus says the LORD, <u>'Heaven is My throne</u>, and the earth is My footstool.'"(NAS)

Matt 5:34 "But I say to you, make no oath at all, either by <u>heaven, for it is the throne of God</u>"

In Ezekiel's vision (Ezek 1:4-28), the throne of God came to him on a cloud at the banks of the river Chebar. This vision contained some of the same elements found in the other visions: the four living creatures, the cherubim, the throne of God and the Lord Himself in the form of a man. Again in the entire tenth chapter of Ezekiel he witnesses <u>the same portable throne room</u> rendering judgment on the city of Jerusalem at the hands of the cherubim.

Daniel also tells of a vision of <u>a throne from which God judges the</u> <u>world</u>. Jesus makes several corroborating comments. In conjunction with John's comments in Revelation it is apparent that this will occur AFTER the Millennial Reign.

*Dan 7:9-10 "I kept looking until **thrones were set up**, and the Ancient of Days took His seat. His vesture was like white snow, and the hair of His head like pure wool. His throne was ablaze with flames, its wheels were a burning fire. 10 "A river of fire was flowing and coming out from before Him. Thousands upon thousands were attending Him, and myriads upon myriads were standing before Him. <u>The court sat, and the books were opened</u>. (NAS)*

*Matt 19:28 And Jesus said to them, "Truly I say to you, that you who have followed Me, in the regeneration **(the resurrection)** <u>when the Son of Man will sit on His glorious throne</u>, you also shall sit upon twelve thrones, judging the twelve tribes of Israel. (NAS)*

Matt 25:31-33 "But when the Son of Man comes in His glory, and all the angels with Him, then <u>He will sit on His glorious throne</u>. 32 "And all the nations will be gathered before Him; and He will separate them from one another, as the shepherd separates the sheep from the goats; 33 and He will put the sheep on His right, and the goats on the left. (NAS)

*Rev 20:11-15 And I saw a **<u>great white throne</u>** and Him who sat upon it, from whose presence earth and heaven **(the physical heavens)** fled away, and no place was found for them. 12 And I saw the dead, the great and the small, <u>standing before the throne,</u> **<u>and books were opened</u>**; and another book was opened, which is the book of life; and the dead were judged from the things which were written in the books, according to their deeds. 13 And the sea gave up the dead which were in it, and death and Hades gave up the dead which were in them; and they were judged, every one of them according to their deeds. 14 And death and Hades were thrown into the lake of fire. This is the second death, the lake of fire. 15 And if anyone's name was not found written in the book of life, he was thrown into the lake of fire. (NAS)*

That Jesus, the Messiah and the Son of David, will sit on <u>an</u> <u>adjacent throne at the right hand of the Father</u> is a frequent theme in the scriptures, especially in Hebrews. (Ps 110:1; Mt 22:44, 26:64; Mk 16:19; Act 2:25-36; Ps 16:8-11; Acts 5:31, 7:55-56; Rom 8:34; Eph 1:19-23; Col 3:1; 1 Peter 3:22; Heb 1:3,1:13; 8:1; 10:12; 12:22)

> *Heb 8:1 Now the main point in what has been said is this: we have such a high priest (Jesus) who has taken <u>His seat at the right hand</u> <u>of the throne of the Majesty</u> in the heavens. (NAS)*

A GREAT CLOUD OF WITNESSES

Another thing we know about Heaven is that it is the present location of the righteous dead. In fact, we are told that "grandma is watching us, so we better behave ☺."

> *Heb 12:1-2 Therefore, since we have so **great a cloud of witnesses** surrounding us, let us also lay aside every encumbrance, and the sin which so easily entangles us, and let us run with endurance the race that is set before us, 2 fixing our eyes on Jesus, the author and perfecter of faith, who for the joy set before Him endured the cross, despising the shame, and <u>has sat down at the right hand of</u> <u>the throne of God</u>. (NAS)*

This "**great cloud of witnesses**" brings us to another revelation about who or what is to be found in Heaven. <u>It is the location of the</u> <u>righteous dead in Christ</u>. As we have outlined earlier, any believer who died/dies after the resurrection of Jesus, went/goes to be with Jesus (2 Cor 5:6-9). Prior to the resurrection of Jesus, the righteous dead dwelt in Sheol. Therefore, <u>Heaven is full of the souls of our dearly departed</u> <u>who, in their lifetime, walked with the Lord</u>. At this point they exist in a spiritual state only, awaiting their own resurrection and glorified bodies at the Second Coming of Christ (1 Cor 15 :20-24).

> *1 Cor 15:20-24 But now <u>Christ has been raised from the dead, the</u> <u>first fruits</u> of those who are asleep. 21 For since by a man came*

death, by a man also came the resurrection of the dead. 22 For as in Adam all die, so also in Christ all shall be made alive. 23 But each in his own order: Christ the first fruits, <u>after that those who are Christ's at His coming</u>, 24 then comes the end, when He delivers up the kingdom to the God and Father, when He has abolished all rule and all authority and power. (NAS)

It is John the Revelator who gives us the most developed and extensive looks into the Throne Room of God. He describes it, its inhabitants, and its "culture" in chapters 1, 3, 4, 5, 6, 7, 8, 12, 14, 16, 19, 20, 21 and 22.

Jesus tells us that there is <u>no human state of marriage in Heaven,</u> but that in Heaven we are like the angels.

Matt 22:29-30 But Jesus answered and said to them, "You are mistaken, not understanding the Scriptures, or the power of God. 30 "For in the resurrection they neither marry, nor are given in marriage, but <u>are like angels in heaven</u>." (NAS)

Heaven is by definition in eternity and not in time. Eternity is not a long time, but rather it is a different state or condition of existence. It is not a natural environment for physical bodies. It is, however, the stated location of the glorified body of Jesus.

*1 Cor 15:39-44 All flesh is not the same flesh, but there is one flesh of men, and another flesh of beasts, and another flesh of birds, and another of fish. 40 **There are also heavenly bodies and earthly bodies, but the glory of the heavenly is one, and the glory of the earthly is another**. 41 There is one glory of the sun, and another glory of the moon, and another glory of the stars; for star differs from star in glory. 42 So also is the resurrection of the dead. It is sown a perishable body, it is raised an imperishable body; 43 it is sown in dishonor, it is raised in glory; it is sown in weakness, it is raised in power; 44 **it is sown a natural body, it is raised a spiritual body**. If there is a natural body, there is also a spiritual body. (NAS)*

Frankly, Heaven is a different world about which we know very little. It contains God (a spirit), the angels (also spirits), Jesus (a resurrected body), the saints who have gone on before (all spirits at this time) and will contain the resurrected bodies of the saints eventually. There is no Biblical reason to expect "mansions of gold on streets of silver" in the sweet by and by. These constructs are metaphorical. What Heaven is really like only Heaven knows ☺.

The Book of Revelation –Chapter Summaries"

THE BOOK OF Revelation offers a <u>unique encapsulation</u> of the events leading up to and including the Eschaton. A summary of the chapters is offered here in order to provide perspective and to help the reader <u>find the evangelical support which is the main purpose of this book</u>. When taken in conjunction with the other scriptures offered herein, the Book of Revelation becomes easier to understand and provides structure for eschatological prophecy as a whole.

I. Rev 1:1-20 - John has a vision of the throne room of God.

II. Rev 2: 1-3:22–Letters to the seven churches of Asia Minor

    a. Ephesus–the "First Love" church–**repent and renew**.

    b. Smyrna–the "Good" church - **just endure**.

    c. Pergamum–Balaam & the Nicolaitans-syncretism–**repent**.

    Syncretism is the idolatrous process of blending pagan religious concepts, rituals and thinking into Christianity or Judaism. It attempts to persuade true believers to adopt religious practices and culture contrary to those approved by God. Balaam taught the Canaanites to defeat the Israelites through syncretism when they could not defeat them in battle.

    d. Thyatira–Jezebel & Gnosticism–deep teaching–**repent**.

    Gnosticism was and is heresy that claims to have "special knowledge" or deep teaching necessary for salvation. The claim is that this knowledge is revealed to only the elect and not available to all. Gnosticism (from the Greek word meaning "to know") purports that its knowledge supersedes or obviates traditional orthodoxy. Included in this are theories such as the Sacred Feminine, The Gospel of Mary Magdalene, The Da Vinci Code, the Gospel of Judas, etc.

    e. Sardis–the "Dead" church–a remnant will be saved–**just endure.**

    f. Philadelphia–the "Powerless, Persecuted" church–**just endure.**

    g. Laodicea–the "Rich, Lukewarm, Vomitous" church–**repent.**

III. Rev 4:1-11 - The Throne of God

    a. Four Living Creatures–defenders of God's holiness and worship

    b. Twenty-four elders–Twelve Tribes and Twelve Apostles

    c. Seven Lamps/Spirits–Messengers–The Spirit of God who has seven attributes (Is 11:2).

        i. Spirit of Wisdom

        ii. Spirit of Understanding

        iii. Spirit of Counsel

        iv. Spirit of Strength

        v. Spirit of Knowledge

        vi. Spirit of Fear of the Lord

        vii. Spirit of Delight in God

    d. The Sea of Glass–the righteous dead awaiting the Second Coming.

IV. Rev 5:1-14–The seven sealed book opened by the Lamb/Lion of Judah.

    a. the commissioning of Jesus

    b. Jesus is worshipped as God.

V. Rev 6:1-8:5 The seven seals and the release of the Four Horsemen of the Apocalypse–The Great Tribulation.

    a. Seal one–a white horse–represents despotic conquerors down through history and, in the Eschaton, the Antichrist.

b. Seal two–a red horse–war

c. Seal three–a black horse–scarcity of food but not oil or wine

d. Seal four–a pale horse ridden by Death, followed by Hades. One fourth of the earth is slain by sword, famine, pestilence and wild beasts.

e. Seal five–the martyrs of the ages call for justice.

f. Seal six–a great earthquake, a blackened sun and a blood red moon, falling stars, fear among all men for the Wrath of God (Jer. 30:7) The wind is stilled. The mountains fall into the valleys–(Rev 16:17-21).

g. An interlude to allow for the sealing of the 144,000 Jews on their foreheads for protection from the Wrath to come and the Rapture of the Tribulation church. The Second Coming is delayed until all have "come in" (2 Pet 3:8-13).

h. Seal seven–The Wrath of God is thrown down upon the earth - thunder, lightning and an earthquake followed by the commissioning of seven angels with <u>seven trumpets</u>. The seventh trumpet is the point at which the Lord comes back and the actual Rapture occurs.

VI. Rev 8:6-11:19 - The seven trumpets–The Wrath of God begins. This is round one of God's Wrath. The bowls make up round two of God's Wrath (See XIII).

a. Trumpet one–hail, fire mixed with blood burns one third of the earth, a third of the trees and all of the grass–recalls the plagues of Egypt.

b. Trumpet two–a burning mountain is thrown into the sea turning one third of it to blood, killing one-third of the fish and destroying one third of the ships–asteroid?

c. Trumpet three–a burning star, Wormwood falls on the earth turning one-third of all rivers and springs bitter, killing many–chemical accident?

d. Trumpet four - sunlight, moonlight and starlight are reduced by one-third, shortening daylight and making even the night-time darker. The vast ash filled skies after the eruption of Mt. Pinatubo and Pompeii come to mind. Three woes come.

e. Trumpet five (First Woe)–Apollyon (Abaddon or Lucifer) looses the fallen angels from the bottomless pit (Abyss) to torment all who do not have the seal. He releases great clouds of smoke filled with locust-like creatures that sting like scorpions. All who are stung by them are tormented for five months but not killed, nor can they find death when they seek it. The locusts look like little armored horses with golden crowns on their heads and faces of men, hair like women and teeth like lions, breastplates like iron and tails like scorpions.

f. Trumpet six–In an effort to engender worldwide repentance, four demons from the Euphrates are released to kill one-third of mankind using 200 million horsemen with fiery breastplates, riding horses with heads of lions breathing deadly fire, smoke and brimstone and tails having snakes' heads with which to do further harm. This is the Second Woe.

VII.   Rev 11:1-14–Two witnesses - The Gentiles tread on the Holy city for forty-two months, the Two Witnesses prophesy from Jerusalem for 1260 days (Great Tribulation) clothed in sackcloth, destroying their attackers with fire from out of their mouths, shutting down the rain, turning waters into blood and smiting the earth with plagues. They represent the Law and the Prophets by which the unsaved world will be judged. Perhaps they are Moses and Elijah (see Mk 9:2-4). After that the beast (Antichrist) will kill them, leaving their bodies in the street for three and one-half days for taunting. Then they will be resurrected and caught up to heaven causing an earthquake in Jerusalem that destroys one-tenth of the city and kills 7,000 people.

a. Trumpet seven (Third Woe)–the coming of Jesus and the remainder of the Wrath of God including an earthquake and a hailstorm.

VIII. Rev 12: 1-17–In the middle of the Tribulation there is a spiritual battle in the heavens and a great dragon with seven heads and ten horns (Satan) is thrown down onto the earth and persecutes Israel full force for three and one-half years.

IX. Rev 13:1-10–The Antichrist defined - seven heads, ten horns, empowered by the dragon (Satan), blasphemous, persuasive, receiving a fatal head wound, reanimated from the dead by Satan (the legend of **Nero Redivivus**), worshipping the dragon (Satan), and having authority for forty-two months. He makes war on the saints and is worshipped by all of mankind that is not sealed for God.

X. Rev 13: 11-18–The False Prophet defined - two horns, speaks like the dragon (Satan), creates an image of the Antichrist to be worshipped by all and gives the image breath and voice, does signs and wonders in the presence of the Antichrist such as calling down fire. He requires all to take the mark on their head or right hand and forbids all to buy or sell without the mark. The number of the Antichrist is 666

XI. Rev 14:1-13 The Lamb is now in view and is accompanied by 144,000 believers. Three angels make announcements. They are:

   a.   The appointed number has now come in,

   b.   Babylon is fallen, and

   c.   Anyone who takes the mark of the beast will suffer the Wrath and be eternally damned.

XII.   Rev 14:14-20 - The Second Coming of Jesus, the harvesting of the saints (Mt 13:38-43), THE RAPTURE of the church (15-16) and the Wrath of God on the earth (round two) (17-20). "Blood to a horse's bridle for 200 miles" represents the enormous "quantity" of judgment.

XIII. Rev 15:1-16:21–The seven bowls of Judgment (the second half of the Wrath of God)

   a.   Bowl one–loathsome and malignant sores are on those with the mark of the beast (like Egyptian boils).

   b.   Bowl two–the sea is turned into blood and everything in it dies (reminiscent of the Exodus).

    c. Bowl three–all rivers and springs are turned into blood and everything in them dies (again reminiscent of the plagues of Egypt).

    d. Bowl four–the sun scorches unrepentant mankind with fire, heat and sunburn.

    e. Bowl five–the Antichrist's throne is attacked, his kingdom darkened and they all gnaw at their tongues in torment (again like Egypt).

    f. Bowl six–the Euphrates is dried up to allow the coming of the kings from the east to march upon Jerusalem. A demonic trinity of demons go out from the mouths of the dragon, the Antichrist and the false prophet to gather the kings of men to battle, luring them with signs and wonder, calling them all to Armageddon (the Plains of Esdraelon and Megiddo).

    g. Bowl seven–lightning, thunder, the greatest earthquake of all times. Babylon is split in three parts, all the cities of the earth fall down, all islands disappear and all mountains fall down (Pangaea restored –and there is a plague of hailstones from heaven.

    h. Rev 17:1-18:24–Babylon (the Harlot) is explained, destroyed and judged.

        i. She lured the men of earth away from God.

        ii. She feasted on the blood of the martyrs.

        iii. She reappeared in new forms in every age.

        iv. She was overcome (defeated) by faith, hope and love over the ages, by Jesus and his saints in the end.

        v. Her demise was sudden, horrible and final. Although we are not yet done with Satan at this point, we are done with Babylon.

XIV. Rev 19:1-20:15– Final events

    a. Jesus is acknowledged in Heaven.

    b. The Marriage Supper is called.

    c. The Second Coming is explained.

    d. The Antichrist and the False Prophet are thrown into Hell.

e. Satan is bound for 1,000 years.

f. The Millennial Reign begins.

g. Satan is released after 1,000 years to test mankind.

h. Satan is thrown into Hell forever.

i. The great White Throne Judgment - all who from the beginning of time to the present do not belong to the Lamb are judged. There is a separation of the "sheep and the goats" from the Millennial Reign. All unbelievers are thrown into Hell for eternity. Death and Hades are also thrown into Hell.

XV.   Rev 21:1-22:5 - The Millennial Kingdom explained.

XVI. Rev 22:6-21–Concluding words of encouragement.

Appendix II

A Time, Times and a Half Time

THE ARAMAIC WORD for "time" ('iddan) as in Daniel 7:25 means "a set period," technically, a year. Context is then used to determine the length of that period. In Biblical prophecy, a "time" is considered to equal a year. In Hebrew, the same word for prophetic "time" (mo'wed or mo'ed) as in Daniel 12:7 clearly means a year.

Dan 7:24-25 'And he will speak out against the Most High and wear down the saints of the Highest One, and he will intend to make alterations in times and in law; and they will be given into his hand for a time, times, and half a time. (NAS)

Dan 12:6-7 And one said to the man dressed in linen, who was above the waters of the river, "How long will it be until the end of these wonders?" 7 And I heard the man dressed in linen, who was above the waters of the river, as he raised his right hand and his left toward heaven, and swore by Him who lives forever that it would be for a time, times, and half a time; and as soon as they finish shattering the power of the holy people, all these events will be completed. (NAS)

A comparison and correlation of prophetic scripture in both the Old and New Testaments removes all doubt as to the time frame being discussed. This is accomplished by the logic of equivalencies.

I.   Rev 12:13-14 tells us that the Antichrist will wage war on the
     saints for **A Time, Times and a Half Time.** The Greek word for
     "time" (kai'ros) also means a set period of time, the length of
     which is determined by context. Other interpretive words could
     be "a season" or" "awhile."

     *And when the dragon saw that he was thrown down to the earth,
     he persecuted the woman who gave birth to the male child. 14 And
     the two wings of the great eagle were given to the woman, in order
     that she might fly into the wilderness to her place, where she was
     nourished for **a time and times and half a time**, from the presence
     of the serpent. (NAS)*

II. Dan 7:23-27 agrees with that assessment indicating that Daniel
     and John are using the terms in the same way.

     *Dan 7:23-27 "Thus he said: 'The fourth beast will be a fourth
     kingdom on the earth, which will be different from all the other
     kingdoms, and it will devour the whole earth and tread it down and
     crush it. 24' As for the ten horns, out of this kingdom ten kings will
     arise; and another will arise after them, and he will be different
     from the previous ones and will subdue three kings. 25'And he will
     speak out against the Most High and wear down the saints of the
     Highest One, and he will intend to make alterations in times and
     in law; and they will be given into his hand for **a time, times, and
     half a time**. 26'But the court will sit for judgment, and his dominion
     will be taken away, annihilated and destroyed forever. 27'Then the
     sovereignty, the dominion, and the greatness of all the kingdoms
     under the whole heaven will be given to the people of the saints of
     the Highest One; His kingdom will be an everlasting kingdom, and
     all the dominions will serve and obey Him.' (NAS)*

III. Rev 11:1-11 indicates that **a time, times, and half a time** is
     equivalent to **forty-two months** and **twelve hundred and sixty
     days.**

     *And there was given me a measuring rod like a staff; and someone
     said, "Rise and measure the temple of God, and the altar, and those*

who worship in it. 2 "And leave out the court which is outside the temple, and do not measure it, for it has been given to the nations; and **they will tread under foot the holy city for forty-two months.** *3 "And I will grant authority to my two witnesses, and* ***they will prophesy for twelve hundred and sixty days****, clothed in sackcloth." 4 These are the two olive trees and the two lampstands that stand before the Lord of the earth. 5 And if anyone desires to harm them, fire proceeds out of their mouth and devours their enemies; and if anyone would desire to harm them, in this manner he must be killed. 6 These have the power to shut up the sky, in order that rain may not fall during the days of their prophesying; and they have power over the waters to turn them into blood, and to smite the earth with every plague, as often as they desire. 7 And when they have finished their testimony, the beast that comes up out of the abyss will make war with them, and overcome them and kill them. 8 And their dead bodies will lie in the street of the great city which mystically is called Sodom and Egypt, where also their Lord was crucified. 9 And those from the peoples and tribes and tongues and nations will look at their dead bodies for three and a half days, and will not permit their dead bodies to be laid in a tomb. 10 And those who dwell on the earth will rejoice over them and make merry; and they will send gifts to one another, because these two prophets tormented those who dwell on the earth. 11 And after the* ***three and a half days*** *the breath of life from God came into them, and they stood on their feet; and great fear fell upon those who were beholding them.* (NAS)

IV. Rev 12:6-7 reconfirms the equivalency with **one thousand two hundred and sixty days.**

And the woman fled into the wilderness where she had a place prepared by God, so that there she might be nourished for ***one thousand two hundred and sixty days****. And I heard the man dressed in linen, who was above the waters of the river, as he raised his right hand and his left toward heaven, and swore by Him who lives forever that it would be for a* ***time, times, and half a time;*** *and as soon as they finish shattering the power of the holy people, all these events will be completed* (NAS)

V. Rev 13:3-7 reconfirms the equivalency with **forty-two months**.

*And I saw one of his heads as if it had been slain, and his fatal wound was healed. And the whole earth was amazed and followed after the beast; 4 and they worshiped the dragon, because he gave his authority to the beast; and they worshiped the beast, saying, "Who is like the beast, and who is able to wage war with him?" 5 And there was given to him a mouth speaking arrogant words and blasphemies; and authority to act for **forty-two months** was given to him. 6 And he opened his mouth in blasphemies against God, to blaspheme His name and His tabernacle, that is, those who dwell in heaven. 7 And it was given to him to make war with the saints and to overcome them; and authority over every tribe and people and tongue and nation was given to him.*

VI. An explanation of the Seventy Weeks of Daniel and its likely calculation is also relevant to this discussion.

*Dan 9:24-27 "**Seventy weeks** have been decreed for your people and your holy city, to finish the transgression, to make an end of sin, to make atonement for iniquity, to bring in everlasting righteousness, to seal up vision and prophecy, and to anoint the most holy place. 25 "So you are to know and discern that from the issuing of a decree to restore and rebuild Jerusalem until Messiah the Prince there will be **seven weeks and sixty-two weeks**; it will be built again, with plaza and moat, even in times of distress. 26 "Then after the sixty-two weeks the Messiah will be cut off and have nothing, and the people of the prince who is to come (the Antichrist) will destroy the city and the sanctuary. And its end will come with a flood; even to the end there will be war; desolations are determined. 27 "And he will make a firm covenant with the many for one week, but in the middle of the week he will put a stop to sacrifice and grain offering; and on the wing of abominations will come **one who makes desolate**, even until a complete destruction, one that is decreed, is poured out on the **one who makes desolate**." (NAS)*

The Seventy Weeks of Daniel prophesied in Daniel 9:24-27 is a much discussed passage. The challenge is to understand the metaphor. As a literal, scientific, non-metaphorical statement, it makes no historical sense. It implies that Jerusalem and the temple would be rebuilt in about sixteen months (sixty-nine literal weeks) from the decree to rebuild and then be destroyed again. That did not happen. The Messiah would have had to come and be "cut off" in about fourteen months (sixty-two literal weeks). This would not be very comforting to Daniel, and yet comforting Daniel is the purpose of Gabriel's visit. These constructs are inconsistent with all historical data and with Daniel 11. It would have made the comments of Jesus, Paul and John meaningless, not to mention erroneous.

The "Seventy weeks" are not actual weeks. They are weeks of years. That is the literal Hebrew meaning of "shib'iym shabu'iym" (seventy sevens, seventy weeks or seventy heptads).The prophecy is a combination of things that are clear and things that are not. The seventy years of the Babylonian captivity is clear in the Hebrew language. Jeremiah 25:11 uses the phrase "shib`iym sha'neh" (seventy years), a term meaning 70 actual years. Jeremiah 29:10 uses the same phrase for seventy years. The seventy weeks in Daniel 9:24 clearly means 490 years based on the language. Seventy weeks is "shib'iym shabu'iym" (seventy sevens, seventy weeks or seventy heptads).The phrase means 70 sevens or 490 time periods. (years). It is interpreted "70 weeks of years" in both the sacred and secular usage of Daniel's day. Context has led scholars over time to interpret this as 490 lunar years.

The **starting point** of the 490 lunar years is open to **MUCH** debate. There are twelve or thirteen workable theories leading to two major interpretations. One theory is that the starting point for the 490 years is based on Cyrus' decree that allowed the Israelites to go home. This causes the 490 lunar years to end NOWHERE in particular. The closest possible interpretation is the time of Antiochus Epiphanes and that theory has been received by many as a likely interpretation. However, that theory doesn't work for Jesus, Paul and John, so it doesn't work for me. They all have the Antichrist as future to themselves and Jesus has the Antiochus Epiphanes events as already come and gone (Mt 24:15).

> *Matt 24:15-18 "Therefore when you see the **abomination of desola-***
> ***tion** which was spoken of through Daniel the prophet, standing in*
> *the holy place (**let the reader understand**), 16 then let those who are*
> *in Judea flee to the mountains; 17 let him who is on the housetop*
> *not go down to get the things out that are in his house; 18 and let*
> *him who is in the field not turn back to get his cloak. (NAS)*

The much more likely imperial decree referenced in Daniel 9:24 as the starting point of the 490 years is the decree by Artaxerxes I, stepson to Esther and friend to Nehemiah, the man whom God sent to restore Jerusalem. In about 445 B.C. Artaxerxes I issued the decree for Jerusalem to be rebuilt and the temple restored. By adding 483 lunar years (sixty-nine weeks of years) to those dates, the timeline would have the Messiah "cut off" at about the time that Jesus was crucified. Adding more support to the eschatological interpretation is the description of what the Messiah in question would actually accomplish when He comes at the end of the sixty-nine weeks. Let's look again at verse 24 from above. He would

a. finish the transgression,
b. make an end of sin,
c. make atonement for iniquity,
d. bring in everlasting righteousness,
e. seal up (fulfill) vision and prophecy, and
f. anoint the most holy place.

As Christians we are committed to the idea that only Jesus by His passion, death and resurrection in circa 29-33 A.D. could accomplish this whole list.

Once again, the calculation of the 490 lunar years is found in the Hebrew words used as outlined above. There will be sixty-nine weeks of weeks (483 lunar years) until the First Coming of the Messiah. There will be one more week of weeks (seven lunar years) until His Second Coming. That's 490 lunar years between the "now" in Daniel 9:24 and the culmination of all things (Dan 9:24). The last week (seven lunar years) concerns the activity of the Antichrist. According to Daniel (and Jesus) the first three and one-half "weeks" of his reign is a period of deceitfulness, followed by a second three and one-half weeks of broken covenant after the abomination that makes desolate (Dan 9:26).

JULIAN CALENDAR CALCULATION

Most scholars agree that the death of Christ happened at the Passover in the month Nisan, in the four thousand seven hundred and forty-sixth year of the Julian period. Four hundred and eighty-three years, reckoned back from the above year, leads us directly to the very month and year in which Ezra had his commission from Artaxerxes Longimanus, King of Persia, (see Ezra 7:9) to restore and rebuild Jerusalem. See the commission in Ezra 7:11-26.

MODERN CALENDAR CALCULATION

The 483 years begins 1 Nisan 445 B.C. (March 14, 445 B.C. according to Nehemiah 2:1-9) and ends 10th Nisan 32 A.D. (Palm Sunday April 6, 32 A.D. according to John 11:55-12:1-16) which period is 173,880 days. Between the sixty-ninth and the seventieth week is a mystery hidden from the Jews - that is, the Church Age, the mechanism by which the Gentiles might be saved (Eph 3:3-12). After this age comes the seventieth week of Daniel. The vision of the seventy weeks of Daniel tells of both the First and the Second Coming of Christ with no comment on the gap in-between (Gen 49:10-11, Isaiah 53:1-12, Micah 5:1-15, Mal 3:1-5, Zech 9: 9-10, 1Peter 1:10-12).

Two final comments might be helpful. First, the reason for the perceived separation between the sixty-ninth week of Daniel and the seventieth week of Daniel is found initially in the information given Daniel by the angel in Daniel 9:24-27. It is he who designates the separation of the last week from the other period. This is further supported by Paul's revelation that the Gentile church age was a mystery hidden in ages and that God would in time re-graft Israel into the vine.

*Eph 3:3-7 That by revelation there was made known to me the mystery, as I wrote before in brief. 4 And by referring to this, when you read you can understand <u>my insight into the mystery of Christ</u>, 5 which in other generations was <u>not made known to the sons of men</u>, as it has now been revealed to His holy apostles and prophets in the Spirit; 6 to be specific, **that the Gentiles are fellow heirs and fellow members of the body, and fellow partakers of the promise in Christ Jesus through the gospel**, 7 of which I was made a minister, according to the gift of God's grace which was given to me according to the working of His power. (NAS)*

The mystery hidden in ages from the Jews was the existence of the Gentile church. It was actually prophesied by many prophets and by God to Abraham, Moses and others, but the Jews had "eyes that could not see and ears that could not hear."

*Rom 11:25-29 For I do not want you, brethren, to be uninformed <u>of this mystery,</u> lest you be wise in your own estimation, that <u>**a partial hardening has happened to Israel until the fullness of the Gentiles has come in**</u>; 26 and thus all Israel will be saved; just as it is written, "The <u>Deliverer will come from Zion</u>, He will remove ungodliness from Jacob." 27 "And this is My covenant with them, When I take away their sins." 28 From the standpoint of the gospel they are enemies for your sake, but <u>from the standpoint of God's choice they are beloved for the sake of the fathers;</u> 29 for <u>the gifts and the calling of God are irrevocable.</u> (NAS)*

Rom 11:17-24 But if <u>some of the branches were broken off</u>, and you, being a wild olive, were grafted in among them and became partaker with them of the rich root of the olive tree, 18 do not be arrogant toward the branches; but if you are arrogant, remember that <u>it is not you who supports the root, but the root supports you.</u> 19 You will say then, "Branches were broken off so that I might be grafted in." 20 Quite right, <u>they were broken off for their unbelief,</u> but you stand by your faith. Do not be conceited, but fear; 21 for <u>if God did not spare the natural branches, neither will He spare you.</u> 22 Behold then the kindness and severity of God; to those who fell, severity, but to you, God's kindness, if you continue in His kindness; otherwise you also will be cut off. 23 And <u>they also,</u>

if they do not continue in their unbelief, will be grafted in; for God is able to graft them in again. 24 For if you were cut off from what is by nature a wild olive tree, and were grafted contrary to nature into a cultivated olive tree, how much more shall these who are the natural branches be grafted into their own olive tree? (NAS)

Second, the reason that many scholars and students of prophecy have been convinced that the Antichrist will come from the people based in the old Roman Empire is found in Daniel 9:26-27. The "prince who is to come" in Dan 9:26 is the Antichrist. The Antichrist's people (his ancestors) are the people group who would destroy Jerusalem in the day that the Messiah would be cut off. Since it was the Romans who had conquered Palestine during Jesus' lifetime and the Roman General Titus who destroyed Jerusalem in 66-70 A.D., the thinking is that the Antichrist would come from what was the old Roman Empire.

Dan 9:26-27 "Then after the sixty-two weeks the Messiah will be cut off and have nothing, and the people of the prince who is to come (the Antichrist) will destroy the city and the sanctuary. And its end will come with a flood; even to the end there will be war; desolations are determined. 27 "And he will make a firm covenant with the many for one week, but in the middle of the week he will put a stop to sacrifice and grain offering; and on the wing of abominations will come one who makes desolate, even until a complete destruction, one that is decreed, is poured out on the one who makes desolate." (NAS)

The Themes of Isaiah

Good News–Gospel: Is 40:9; 41:27; 52:7; 60:6; 61:1 (100+ NT references)

- Comfort (Naham): Is 40:1, Jonah 3:9-10, 4:2

Former things, new things: Is 41:22, 26; 42:9; 43:18-19; 46:9; 48:3-6; 65:16-17

Servant of the Lord: Is 42:1-9; 49:1-7; 50:4-9; 52:13-53:12; 61:1-2

Favorable Year of the Lord: Is 42: 6-7; 49:8; 61:1-2; Luke 4:16-21

Sovereignty: Is 40:12-27; 42:5-9; 45:1-13 calamity; 46:1-13

- Monotheism: Is 40:19-20; 44:6-20; 45:22-23; 46:9
- Taunting of the gods: Is 41:21-24; 46:1-2

Highway in the Desert: Is 7:26; 11:16; 40:1-5; 42:13-16; 49:11; Pro 15:19

- Restoration of Israel: Is 35:1-10; 49:1-26; 52:1-15; 54: 1-17; 55:1-13; 62:1-12, 66:18-23; Jer 31:9, 21
- Restoration of Egypt and Assyria: Is 19:18-25
- Exodus imagery:Is 10: 26; 11:15; 16:43; 44:27; 48:20-22; 49:24-26; 50:2; 51:10; 63:11-13; 64:1-4

Mountains and valleys rearranged, Pangaea: Is 2:2-4, 12-22; 5:25; 40:1-5; 41:15; 42:13-15; 49:11; 54:10; 64:1-4; 65:7; Jer 4:23-29, Ezek 38:17-20; Amos 9:11-13, Zech 14

Blind eyes and deaf ears: Is 1:15; 5:21; 6:9-11; 11:1-3; 29: 9-10, 18; 30:20-21; 32:1-4; 33:14-15; 35:1-5; 37:17; 42:13-20; 43:8-20; 44:18; 52:8; 59:10; Jer 5:21; Ez 40:4; 44:5; Micah 3:6-7; Amos 8:11; Mt 13:15; 16:13; Mk 8:18; Lk 24:16, 31; Jn 12:40; Acts 28:27; Rom 8:11; Eph 1:18

Nations: Is 2:2-4, 11:10-12, 25:6-7, 42:6, 49:6, 55:4, 56:7, 60:3, 62:2, 66:18

God's discipline of his beloved children: Is 48:1-2, 50:1-3; 52: 3; Ps 44:9-16; Heb 12

True fast: Is 58:1-14; Zch 7:1-14; 8:16-19
- justice issues: Isaiah 1:10-27; 5:7-8; 9:7; 10:1-2; 16:5; 28:6; Chapters 16-17; 30:18; 33:1-18; 42:3-4; 56:1, 11; 57:17; 59:1-21; 61:8; Jer 5:26-31; 7:1-11; 22:3; Mic 6:8; Mal 3:1-5

Last things:
- Day of vengeance: Is 2:12; 10:3; 13:1-13; 17:1-14; Chapters 21-23; 30:6-33; 48:8; 61:2; 63:1-19; 2 Peter 3: 9-10
- Return of Christ: Is 24:1-23; 27:1-13; 61:1-11, Zech 14:1-8; Rev 11:15-19; Mt 24:27-44; Mk 13:24-37; Lk 21:25-36; 1Cor 15:20-28, 51-58; 2Tim 4:7-8; Rev 19:11-21; Is 63:1-6; 1Thes 4:13-18; Mt 13 (wheat & tares), Dan 7
- Millennial Reign: Is 2:2-4; 11:1-16; 35:1-10; 55:9-13; 60:1-22; 61:1-11; 62:1-12; 65:17-25; Zech 14: 9- 21; Rev 20:1-9; Rev 5:9-10
- Judgment - Treasures: Mt 6: 19-21; 1Cor 3:12-15; Jas 5:1-6; 2Thes 1:5-10
- First Judgment: 2Cor 5:10; Heb 9:27; 1Pet 4:17
- Second Judgment: Rev 20:11-15; Heb 9:27; Mt 25:31-46
- Hell: Is 66:24; Mt 10:28; 18:8; 25:41-46; Mk 9:42-50; 2Pet 2:4; Rev 14:11; 20:10, 14-15

Pleasant Word

Printed in the United States
100803LV00004B/205-342/A

9 781414 111292